Britain's Railways

2nd Edition

Atlas of Train Operating Companies

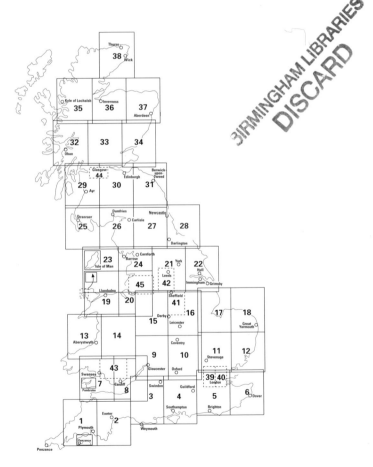

Ian Allan
PUBLISHING

INTRODUCTION

In 1995 the then Conservative Government launched the first of the privatised Train Operating Companies on to a largely unsympathetic railway industry and country. Over the next two years, up to the election of 1 May 1997, the whole of Britain's railway passenger business was to pass into private ownership, with some 25 companies inheriting the previously integrated national network. Some of these new franchises — such as ScotRail or Island Line on the Isle of Wight — were relatively simple, others — most notably Virgin Cross Country — were highly complex.

The first edition of this atlas was produced in 2000; whilst not being without its errors it did show to some effect the complexity of the contemporary railway network. In the six years since the first edition was prepared there has been a considerable number of changes in the franchisees. Gone are, for example, Thameslink and Thames Trains, whilst the First Great(er) Western franchise has, for example, expanded to include much of the erstwhile Thames Trains' and Wessex Trains' operations. Drawing upon the criticism of the first edition and the latest changes to the franchisees, this new edition portrays the railway industry as it exists in the middle of 2006.

In producing the book, all franchised services have been included with two notable exceptions: the ScotRail sleeper service to Euston and the Gatwick Express service from Victoria to Gatwick station. In both cases to have included the services would have added significantly to the complexity of the lines over which they operate and, in the case of the latter, there is every likelihood at the time of writing that the franchise will be terminated and incorporated within an extended Southern franchise.

In terms of the new edition, greater differentiation has been included between Network and non-Network services; the latter are now shown as a thin brown line irrespective of whether they form part of the heritage sector or the commercial non-Network sector (such as Eurostar). In addition, the use of smaller dots for stations should allow for greater clarity as to which operators use each individual station. The prime user or manager of each station recorded is listed within the index and readers should use the index for cross-referencing with the actual entries on the maps. The frequency by which some operators use individual stations isn't indicated — to do so would be virtually impossible with cartography on this scale — and individual TOCs may use a station for nor no more than perhaps one train a week. We hope that we have identified all such irregular use but the occasional quirk of the timetable may well, unfortunately, have been missed.

Readers will appreciate that, given the scale of the atlas and the complexity of the TOC operations at major intersections (such as Reading and Birmingham) it is not possible to illustrate precisely the junction details, but the overall relationship is, as far as possible, correct. For a more detailed analysis of the contemporary railway network — and in particular freight terminals — readers are referred to the OPC / compiled by S. K. Baker.

Every effort has been made to show all passenger services except as detailed above. If there are any errors, the publishers will welcome notification so that changes can be incorporated into the next edition of this book.

First published 2000
Second Edition 2006

ISBN (10) 0 7110 3138 X
ISBN (13) 978 0 3138 8

Published by Ian Allan Publishing

an imprint of Ian Allan Publishing Ltd, Hersham, Surrey, KT12 4RG.
Printed by Ian Allan Printing Ltd, Hersham, Surrey, KT12 4RG.

Code: 0607/

Visit the Ian Allan Publishing web site at:
www.ianallanpublishing.com

Cartography by Maidenhead Cartographic Services Ltd

Cover images by Brian Morrison

K E Y

Arriva Trains Wales	————————
Arriva Trains Wales (to open)	- - - - - - - - - - - - - -
Central Trains	————————
Chiltern	————————
c2c	————————
First Capital Connect	————————
First Greater Western	————————
First Trans Pennine Express	————————
Freight	————————
G.N.E.R.	————————
Hull Trains	————————
Island Line	————————
Mersey Electric	————————
Midland Main line	————————
Northern Trains	————————
'one'	————————
Other Passenger Lines	————————
Other Passenger Lines (Proposed)	- - - - - - - - - - - - -
Other Passenger Lines (Tunnel)	· · · · · · · · · · · · ·
Scotrail	————————
Scotrail (to open)	- - - - - - - - - - - - - -
Silverlink	————————
South Eastern	————————
Southern	
South West Trains	
Virgin Cross Country	
Virgin West Coast	

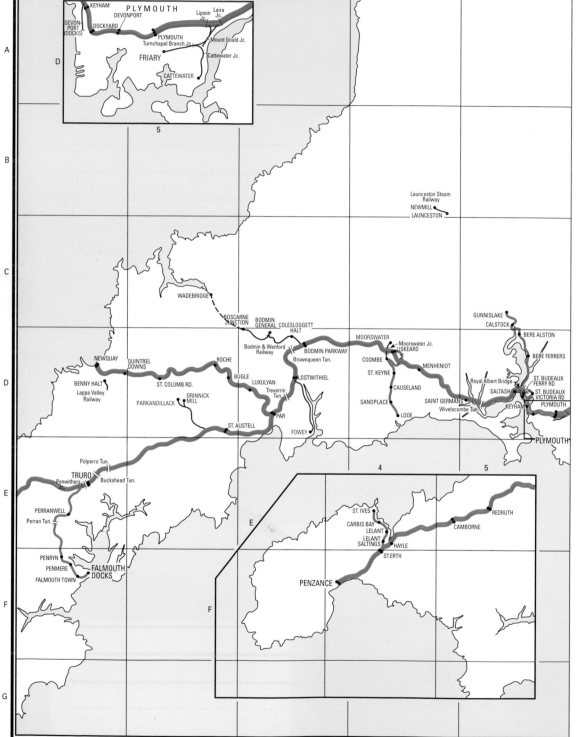

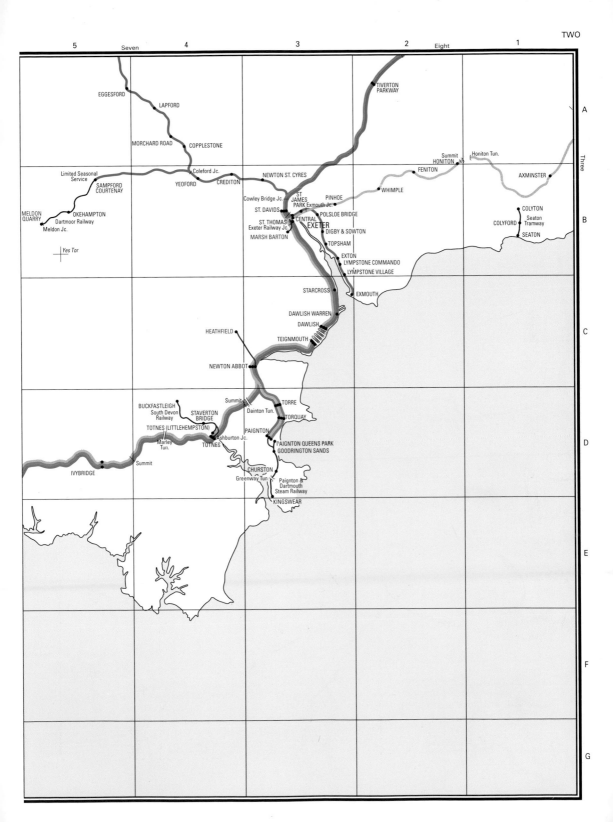

EGGESFORD

LAPFORD

MORCHARD ROAD   COPPLESTONE

Limited Seasonal
Service   Coleford Jc.
SAMPFORD
COURTENAY   YEOFORD   CREDITON   NEWTON ST. CYRES

Cowley Bridge Jc.
MELDON
QUARRY   OKEHAMPTON   ST. DAVIDS
Dartmoor Railway   ST. JAMES
PARK   Exmouth Jc.
Meldon Jc.   ST. THOMAS   CENTRAL   POLSLOE BRIDGE
Exeter Railway Jc.   EXETER   DIGBY & SOWTON
Yes Tor   MARSH BARTON   TOPSHAM
EXTON
LYMPSTONE COMMANDO
LYMPSTONE VILLAGE

STARCROSS   EXMOUTH

DAWLISH WARREN

DAWLISH

HEATHFIELD   TEIGNMOUTH

NEWTON ABBOT

Summit   TORRE
BUCKFASTLEIGH   Dainton Tun.
South Devon   STAVERTON   TORQUAY
Railway   BRIDGE
TOTNES (LITTLEHEMPSTON)   PAIGNTON
Marley   Ashburton Jc.
Tun.   TOTNES   PAIGNTON QUEENS PARK
GOODRINGTON SANDS
IVYBRIDGE   Summit
CHURSTON
Greenway Tun.   Paignton &
Dartmouth
Steam Railway
KINGSWEAR

TIVERTON
PARKWAY

Summit   Honiton Tun.
HONITON
FENITON   AXMINSTER

WHIMPLE   COLYTON
COLYFORD   Seaton
Tramway
PINHOE   SEATON

Three

A

B

C

D

E

F

G

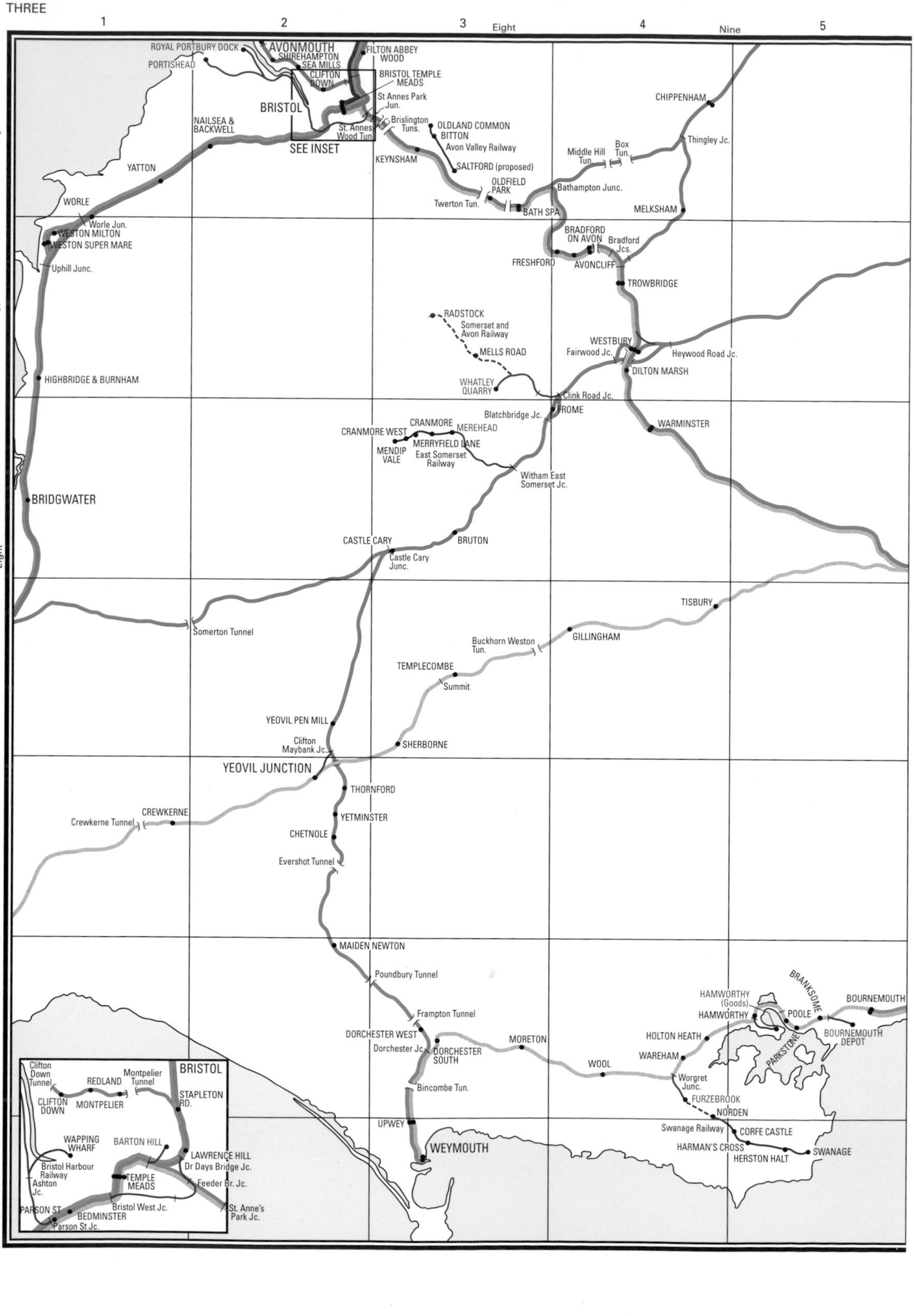
1
2
3
Eight
4
Nine
5
A
B
C
D
E
F
G
Eight
Two
ROYAL PORTBURY DOCK
PORTISHEAD
AVONMOUTH
SHIREHAMPTON
SEA MILLS
CLIFTON DOWN
FILTON ABBEY WOOD
BRISTOL TEMPLE MEADS
St Annes Park Jun.
BRISTOL
Brislington Tuns.
St. Annes Wood Tun.
SEE INSET
NAILSEA & BACKWELL
YATTON
KEYNSHAM
OLDLAND COMMON
BITTON
Avon Valley Railway
SALTFORD (proposed)
OLDFIELD PARK
Twerton Tun.
BATH SPA
Bathampton Junc.
Middle Hill Tun.
Box Tun.
CHIPPENHAM
Thingley Jc.
MELKSHAM
WORLE
Worle Jun.
WESTON MILTON
WESTON SUPER MARE
Uphill Junc.
BRADFORD ON AVON
Bradford Jcs.
FRESHFORD
AVONCLIFF
TROWBRIDGE
RADSTOCK
Somerset and Avon Railway
MELLS ROAD
WESTBURY
Fairwood Jc.
Heywood Road Jc.
DILTON MARSH
HIGHBRIDGE & BURNHAM
WHATLEY QUARRY
Clink Road Jc.
Blatchbridge Jc.
FROME
WARMINSTER
CRANMORE WEST
CRANMORE
MEREHEAD
MERRYFIELD LANE
MENDIP VALE
East Somerset Railway
Witham East Somerset Jc.
BRIDGWATER
CASTLE CARY
Castle Cary Junc.
BRUTON
TISBURY
Somerton Tunnel
Buckhorn Weston Tun.
GILLINGHAM
TEMPLECOMBE
Summit
YEOVIL PEN MILL
Clifton Maybank Jc.
SHERBORNE
YEOVIL JUNCTION
THORNFORD
CREWKERNE
Crewkerne Tunnel
YETMINSTER
CHETNOLE
Evershot Tunnel
MAIDEN NEWTON
Poundbury Tunnel
Frampton Tunnel
DORCHESTER WEST
Dorchester Jc.
DORCHESTER SOUTH
MORETON
WOOL
Bincombe Tun.
UPWEY
WEYMOUTH
HAMWORTHY (Goods)
HAMWORTHY
BRANKSOME
POOLE
BOURNEMOUTH
BOURNEMOUTH DEPOT
HOLTON HEATH
WAREHAM
PARKSTONE
Worgret Junc.
FURZEBROOK
NORDEN
Swanage Railway
CORFE CASTLE
HARMAN'S CROSS
HERSTON HALT
SWANAGE
Clifton Down Tunnel
REDLAND
Montpelier Tunnel
BRISTOL
CLIFTON DOWN
MONTPELIER
STAPLETON RD.
WAPPING WHARF
BARTON HILL
LAWRENCE HILL
Dr Days Bridge Jc.
Bristol Harbour Railway
Ashton Jc.
TEMPLE MEADS
Feeder Br. Jc.
PARSON ST
BEDMINSTER
Bristol West Jc.
St. Anne's Park Jc.
Parson St Jc.

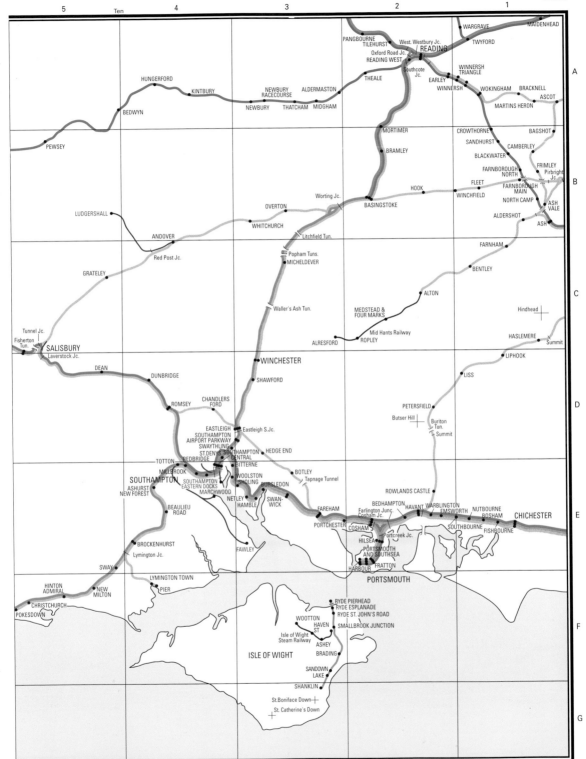

5   Ten   4   3   2   1

A
B
C
D
E
F
G

MAIDENHEAD
WARGRAVE
TWYFORD
PANGBOURNE
TILEHURST
West. Westbury Jc.
Oxford Road Jc.
READING WEST
Southcote Jc.
READING
WINNERSH
TRIANGLE
EARLEY
WINNERSH
WOKINGHAM
BRACKNELL
ASCOT
MARTINS HERON
THEALE
NEWBURY
RACECOURSE
ALDERMASTON
HUNGERFORD
KINTBURY
NEWBURY THATCHAM MIDGHAM
BEDWYN
MORTIMER
BRAMLEY
CROWTHORNE
SANDHURST
BLACKWATER
CAMBERLEY
BAGSHOT
FRIMLEY
Pirbright
Jc.
FARNBOROUGH
NORTH
FARNBOROUGH
MAIN
NORTH CAMP
ASH
VALE
ALDERSHOT
ASH
PEWSEY
HOOK
FLEET
WINCHFIELD
Worting Jc.
BASINGSTOKE
OVERTON
WHITCHURCH
Litchfield Tun.
FARNHAM
BENTLEY
LUDGERSHALL
ANDOVER
Red Post Jc.
Popham Tuns.
MICHELDEVER
ALTON
Hindhead
GRATELEY
Waller's Ash Tun.
MEDSTEAD &
FOUR MARKS
HASLEMERE
Summit
Tunnel Jc.
Fisherton
Tun.
SALISBURY
Laverstock Jc.
Mid Hants Railway
ALRESFORD ROPLEY
LIPHOOK
DEAN
DUNBRIDGE
WINCHESTER
SHAWFORD
LISS
PETERSFIELD
ROMSEY
CHANDLERS
FORD
Butser Hill
Buriton
Tun.
Summit
EASTLEIGH
SOUTHAMPTON
AIRPORT PARKWAY
SWAYTHLING
ST.DENYS SOUTHAMPTON
CENTRAL
Eastleigh S.Jc.
HEDGE END
TOTTON
REDBRIDGE
BITTERNE
MILLBROOK
SOUTHAMPTON
SOUTHAMPTON
EASTERN DOCKS
MARCHWOOD
WOOLSTON
SHOLING
BURSLEDON
BOTLEY
Tapnage Tunnel
ASHURST
NEW FOREST
NETLEY
HAMBLE
SWAN-
WICK
FAREHAM
ROWLANDS CASTLE
BEDHAMPTON
HAVANT WARBLINGTON
EMSWORTH
NUTBOURNE
BOSHAM
CHICHESTER
BEAULIEU
ROAD
PORTCHESTER
Farlington Junc.
Cosham Jc.
COSHAM
Portcreek Jc.
SOUTHBOURNE
FISHBOURNE
BROCKENHURST
Lymington Jc.
FAWLEY
HILSEA
PORTSMOUTH
AND SOUTHSEA
HARBOUR FRATTON
SWAY
LYMINGTON TOWN
PIER
PORTSMOUTH
HINTON
ADMIRAL
NEW
MILTON
CHRISTCHURCH
POKESDOWN
RYDE PIERHEAD
RYDE ESPLANADE
RYDE ST. JOHN'S ROAD
SMALLBROOK JUNCTION
WOOTTON
HAVEN
ST
Isle of Wight
Steam Railway
ASHEY
BRADING
ISLE OF WIGHT
SANDOWN
LAKE
SHANKLIN
St.Boniface Down
St. Catherine's Down

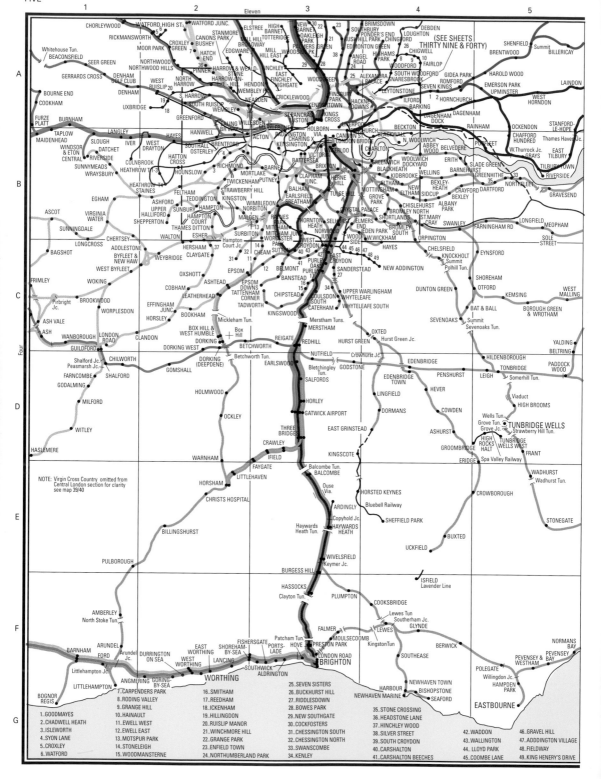

BATTLESBRIDGE

WOODHAM FERRERS

FAMBRIDGE

ALTHORNE

BURNHAM ON CROUCH

WICKFORD

HOCKLEY

ROCHFORD

RAYLEIGH

PRITTLEWELL

VICTORIA

THORPE BAY

BASILDON

PITSEA

BENFLEET

LEIGH ON SEA

CHALKWELL

CENTRAL

EAST WESTCLIFF

PIG'S BAY

SHOEBURYNESS

Canvey Island

THAMESHAVEN

SOUTHEND- ON- SEA

A

Hoo Jc.

HIGHAM

Rochester Br. Jc.

Higham Tnl.

Fort Pitt Tun.

Strood Tnl.

STROOD

THAMES PORT

SHEERNESS- ON-SEA

QUEENBOROUGH

MARGATE

BROADSTAIRS

DUMPTON PARK

WESTGATE-ON-SEA

BIRCHINGTON- ON-SEA

RAMSGATE

B

CUXTON

GILLINGHAM

Gillingham Tun.

Chatham Tun.

RAINHAM

SWALE

King's Ferry Bri.

Minster West Jc.

CHESTFIELD & SWALECLIFFE

WHITSTABLE

HERNE BEY

Minster East Jc.

Minster South Jc.

MINSTER

HALLING

SNODLAND

CHATHAM

ROCHESTER

Western Jc.

Eastern Jc.

NEWINGTON

KEMSLEY

SITTINGBOURNE

TEYNHAM

FAVERSHAM

Faversham Jc.

SELLING

Selling Tun.

WEST

CANTERBURY

EAST

STURRY

BEKESBOURNE

SANDWICH

DEAL

C

NEW HYTHE

AYLESFORD

EAST MALLING

Preston Hall Tuns.

BARMING

BARRACKS

WEST

EAST FARLEIGH

BEARSTED

HOLLINGBOURNE

HARRIETSHAM

LENHAM

CHARING

CHILHAM

CHARTHAM

ADISHAM

AYLESHAM

SNOWDOWN

EYTHORNE

East Kent Light R.

WALMER

MARTIN MILL

WATERINGBURY

MAIDSTONE

MARDEN

STAPLEHURST

HEADCORN

PLUCKLEY

WYE

ASHFORD INTERNATIONAL

SHEPHERDS WELL

Lydden Tun.

KEARSNEY

Buckland Jc.

Charlton Tun.

Harb. Tun.

PRIORY

Guston Tun.

DOVER

D

Saltwood Tun.

Shakespeare Tun.

WESTENHANGER

Sandling Tun.

SANDLING

HYTHE

FOLKESTONE WEST

CENT.

HARB.

Martello Tun.

FOLKESTONE

Abbotscliffe Tun.

To France

HAM STREET

TENTERDEN TOWN

ROLVENDEN

Kent & East Sussex Railway

WITTERSHAM ROAD

NORTHIAM

BODIAM

APPLEDORE

BURMARSH ROAD HALT (Schools only)

DYMCHURCH

ST MARYS BAY

Romney, Hythe & Dymchurch Railway

RYE

NEW ROMNEY

ROMNEY SANDS

DUNGENESS

E

Mountfield Tun.

WINCHELSEA

DUNGENESS POWER STATION

BATTLE

CROWHURST

DOLEHAM

THREE OAKS

Bopeep Tunnel

Ore Tun.

ORE

WEST ST. LEONARDS

BEXHILL

COLLINGTON

Bopeep Jc.

ST LEONARDS WARRIOR SQUARE

Mount Pleasant Tun.

HASTINGS

Hastings Tun

COODEN BEACH

F

G

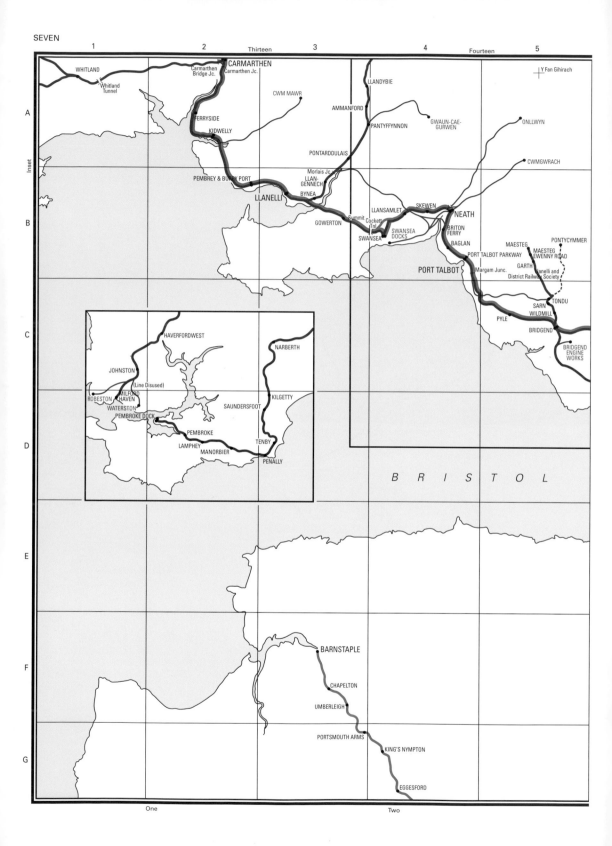

SEVEN

Thirteen Fourteen

1 2 3 4 5

WHITLAND
Whitland Tunnel
Carmarthen Bridge Jc.
Carmarthen Jc.
CARMARTHEN

CWM MAWR

LLANDYBIE

AMMANFORD

GWAUN-CAE-GURWEN

ONLLWYN

FERRYSIDE

KIDWELLY

PANTYFFYNNON

PONTARDDULAIS

CWMGWRACH

PEMBREY & BURRY PORT

Morlais Jc.
LLAN-GENNECH
BYNEA

LLANELLI

LLANSAMLET
SKEWEN
NEATH

GOWERTON

Summit
Cockett Tnl

SWANSEA DOCKS
BRITON FERRY

SWANSEA

BAGLAN

MAESTEG

PONTYCYMMER

MAESTEG EWENNY ROAD

PORT TALBOT PARKWAY

GARTH

PORT TALBOT

Margam Junc.

Llanelli and District Railway Society

TONDU

SARN WILDMILL

PYLE

BRIDGEND

BRIDGEND ENGINE WORKS

Y Fan Gihirach

Inset

HAVERFORDWEST

NARBERTH

JOHNSTON

(Line Disused)

MILFORD HAVEN

ROBESTON

WATERSTON

PEMBROKE DOCK

KILGETTY

SAUNDERSFOOT

PEMBROKE

TENBY

LAMPHEY

MANORBIER

PENALLY

B R I S T O L

BARNSTAPLE

CHAPELTON

UMBERLEIGH

PORTSMOUTH ARMS

KING'S NYMPTON

EGGESFORD

One Two

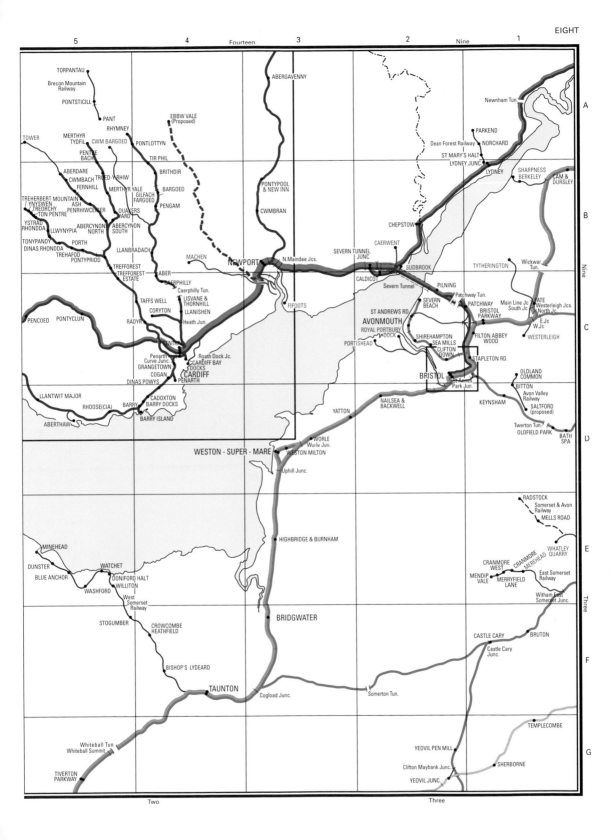

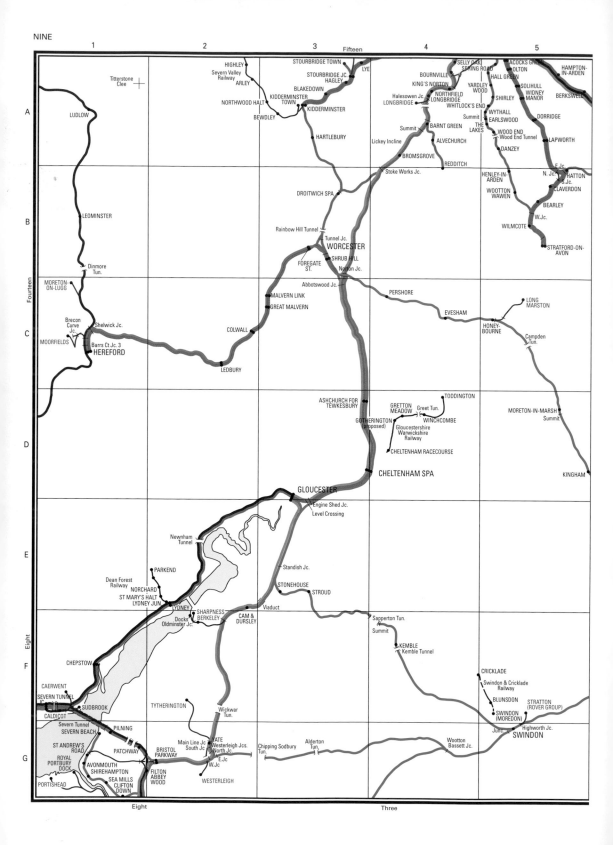

TITTERSTONE CLEE

LUDLOW

HIGHLEY
Severn Valley Railway
ARLEY
NORTHWOOD HALT
KIDDERMINSTER TOWN
BEWDLEY
KIDDERMINSTER

STOURBRIDGE TOWN   LYE
STOURBRIDGE JC.
HAGLEY
BLAKEDOWN

HALESOWEN JC.   LONGBRIDGE
Summit
Lickey Incline
Stoke Works Jc.

SELLY OAK   ACOCKS GREEN
SPRING ROAD   OLTON
BOURNVILLE   HALL GREEN   HAMPTON-IN-ARDEN
KING'S NORTON   YARDLEY WOOD   SOLIHULL   WIDNEY MANOR   BERKSWELL
NORTHFIELD   SHIRLEY
LONGBRIDGE   WHITLOCK'S END   WYTHALL   DORRIDGE
BARNT GREEN   EARLSWOOD
Summit   THE LAKES
ALVECHURCH   WOOD END   Wood End Tunnel   LAPWORTH
BROMSGROVE   DANZEY
REDDITCH

LEOMINSTER

DINMORE Tun.

MORETON-ON-LUGG

Brecon Curve Jc.   Shelwick Jc.
MOORFIELDS
Barrs Ct Jc. 3
HEREFORD

HARTLEBURY

DROITWICH SPA

Rainbow Hill Tunnel
Tunnel Jc.
WORCESTER
FOREGATE ST.   SHRUB HILL
Norton Jc.
Abbotswood Jc.

MALVERN LINK
GREAT MALVERN

COLWALL

LEDBURY

PERSHORE

EVESHAM

HONEY-BOURNE

LONG MARSTON

Campden Tun.

HENLEY-IN-ARDEN
E. Jc.
N. Jc.   HATTON
S. Jc.
CLAVERDON
WOOTTON WAWEN
BEARLEY
W. Jc.
WILMCOTE
STRATFORD-ON-AVON

ASHCHURCH FOR TEWKESBURY

GRETTON   Greet Tun.   TODDINGTON
GOTHERINGTON   WINCHCOMBE
(proposed)   Gloucestershire Warwickshire Railway
CHELTENHAM RACECOURSE

MORETON-IN-MARSH
Summit

KINGHAM

CHELTENHAM SPA

GLOUCESTER
Engine Shed Jc.
Level Crossing

Newnham Tunnel

PARKEND
Dean Forest Railway
NORCHARD
ST MARY'S HALT
LYDNEY JUN   LYDNEY
Docks   SHARPNESS
Oldminster Jc.   BERKELEY

Standish Jc.

STONEHOUSE   STROUD

CAM & DURSLEY

Viaduct

Sapperton Tun.
Summit

KEMBLE
Kemble Tunnel

CHEPSTOW

CAERWENT
SEVERN TUNNEL JC.
CALDICOT   SUDBROOK

Severn Tunnel
SEVERN BEACH   PILNING
ST ANDREW'S ROAD
ROYAL PORTBURY DOCK   PATCHWAY
AVONMOUTH   BRISTOL PARKWAY
PORTISHEAD   SHIREHAMPTON
SEA MILLS
CLIFTON DOWN
FILTON ABBEY WOOD

TYTHERINGTON

Wickwar Tun.

Main Line Jc.   TATE
South Jc.   Westerleigh Jcs.
North Jc.
E. Jc.
W. Jc.
WESTERLEIGH

Chipping Sodbury Tun.

Alderton Tun.

Wootton Bassett Jc.

CRICKLADE
Swindon & Cricklade Railway
BLUNSDON
SWINDON   STRATTON
(MOREDON)   (ROVER GROUP)
Junc   Highworth Jc.
SWINDON

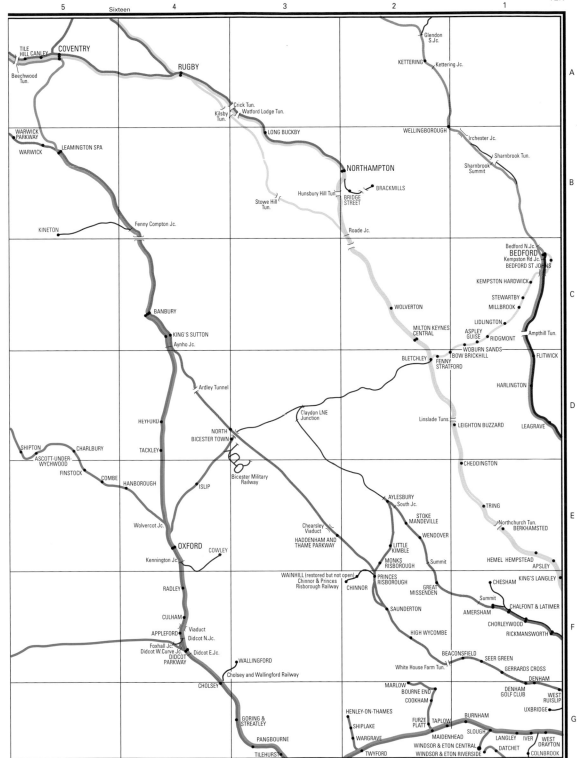

5   Sixteen   4   3   2   1

A

B

C

D

E

F

G

TILE HILL CANLEY
COVENTRY
Beechwood Tun.
RUGBY
Crick Tun.
Kilsby Tun.   Watford Lodge Tun.
LONG BUCKBY
WARWICK PARKWAY
WARWICK
LEAMINGTON SPA
NORTHAMPTON
BRACKMILLS
Hunsbury Hill Tun.   BRIDGE STREET
Stowe Hill Tun.
KINETON
Fenny Compton Jc.
Roade Jc.
Glendon S.Jc.
KETTERING   Kettering Jc.
WELLINGBOROUGH   Irchester Jc.
Sharnbrook Tun.
Sharnbrook Summit
Bedford N.Jc.
Kempston Rd Jc.
BEDFORD
BEDFORD ST JOHNS
KEMPSTON HARDWICK
STEWARTBY
MILLBROOK
LIDLINGTON
ASPLEY GUISE   RIDGMONT   Ampthill Tun.
WOBURN SANDS
BOW BRICKHILL   FLITWICK
WOLVERTON
MILTON KEYNES CENTRAL
BANBURY
KING'S SUTTON
Aynho Jc.
BLETCHLEY
FENNY STRATFORD
HARLINGTON
Ardley Tunnel
HEYFORD
NORTH BICESTER TOWN
Claydon LNE Junction
Linslade Tuns.   LEIGHTON BUZZARD
LEAGRAVE
SHIPTON   CHARLBURY
ASCOTT-UNDER-WYCHWOOD
FINSTOCK   COMBE
TACKLEY
Bicester Military Railway
CHEDDINGTON
HANBOROUGH   ISLIP
AYLESBURY   South Jc.
STOKE MANDEVILLE
TRING
Northchurch Tun.
BERKHAMSTED
Wolvercot Jc.
Chearsley Viaduct
HADDENHAM AND THAME PARKWAY
WENDOVER
OXFORD   COWLEY
Kennington Jc.
LITTLE KIMBLE
MONKS RISBOROUGH   Summit
HEMEL HEMPSTEAD   APSLEY
RADLEY
WAINHILL (restored but not open)
Chinnor & Princes Risborough Railway   CHINNOR
PRINCES RISBOROUGH
GREAT MISSENDEN
CHESHAM   KING'S LANGLEY
CULHAM
SAUNDERTON
Summit
AMERSHAM   CHALFONT & LATIMER
CHORLEYWOOD
APPLEFORD   Viaduct   Didcot N.Jc.
Foxhall Jc.
Didcot W.Curve Jc.   Didcot E.Jc.
DIDCOT PARKWAY
HIGH WYCOMBE
RICKMANSWORTH
WALLINGFORD
BEACONSFIELD
SEER GREEN
White House Farm Tun.   GERRARDS CROSS
DENHAM
CHOLSEY
Cholsey and Wallingford Railway
MARLOW
BOURNE END
COOKHAM
DENHAM GOLF CLUB
WEST RUISLIP
UXBRIDGE
GORING & STREATLEY
HENLEY-ON-THAMES
FURZE PLATT   TAPLOW
BURNHAM
PANGBOURNE
SHIPLAKE
SLOUGH   LANGLEY   IVER
WEST DRAYTON
WARGRAVE
MAIDENHEAD
WINDSOR & ETON CENTRAL   DATCHET
COLNBROOK
TILEHURST
TWYFORD
WINDSOR & ETON RIVERSIDE

1 2 3 4 Seventeen 5

WANSFORD
FERRY MEADOWS
Longueville Jc.
New England Sidings
PETERBOROUGH
WHITEMOOR
Grassmoor Jc.
Whitemoor West Jc.
East Jc.
March S.Jc.
Yarwell Jc.
ORTON MERE
PETERBOROUGH NENE VALLEY
Nene Valley Railway
WHITTLESEA
MARCH

A

MANEA
LITTLEPORT
LAKENHEATH
BRANDON

Ely West Jct.
SHIPPEA HILL

ELY
Sutton Branch Jc.
Dock Jc.

B

HUNTINGDON
FEN DRAYTON
WATERBEACH
KENNETT
Chippenham Jc.
NEWMARKET
Warren Hill Tunnel

Line out of use

ST. NEOTS
Coldham Lane Jc
CAMBRIDGE
DULLINGHAM

C

Shepreth Branch Jc.
SHELFORD

BEDFORD N.Jc.
BEDFORD
Kempston Rd Jc.
BEDFORD ST JOHNS
SANDY
FOXTON
SHEPRETH
WHITTLESFORD

KEMPSTON HARDWICK
STEWARTBY
MILLBROOK
BIGGLESWADE
MELDRETH
GREAT CHESTERFORD

D

Ampthill Tun.
ARLESEY
ASHWELL & MORDEN
ROYSTON
Littlebury Tunnel
Audley End Tunnel

FLITWICK
BALDOCK
LETCHWORTH
AUDLEY END
NEWPORT

HARLINGTON
HITCHIN

E

LEAGRAVE
ELSENHAM
Summit
STANSTED AIRPORT

LUTON AIRPORT PARKWAY
STEVENAGE
STANSTED MOUNTFITCHET
BRAINTREE
LUTON
KNEBWORTH
BISHOP'S STORTFORD
BRAINTREE FREEPORT
CRESSING

Welwyn N.Tun.
WATTON-AT-STONE
WHITE NOTLEY
Welwyn S.Tun.
SAWBRIDGEWORTH

HARPENDEN
Welwyn Viaduct
WELWYN NORTH
WARE
HARLOW MILL
HATFIELD PEVEREL

F

WELWYN GDN. CITY
HERTFORD NORTH
EAST
ST. MARGARETS
HARLOW TOWN

HEMEL HEMPSTEAD
HATFIELD
BAYFORD
RYE HOUSE
ROYDON
ST ALBANS
ST ALBANS ABBEY
Ponsbourne Tun.
Broxbourne Jc.
CHELMSFORD
APSLEY
PARK STREET
WELHAM GREEN
BROXBOURNE

1. THEOBALDS GROVE
2. TURKEY STREET
3. SOUTHBURY
4. BUSH HILL PARK
5. ENFIELD CHASE
6. ENFIELD TOWN
7. OAKLEIGH PARK
8. CROXLEY
9. WATFORD
10. WATFORD HIGH STREET

CUFFLEY
NORTH WEALD
ONGAR
KING'S LANGLEY
HOW WOOD
BROOKMANS PARK
Pilot Development
POTTERS BAR
CREWS HILL
CHESHUNT
BRICKET WOOD
RADLETT
Potters Bar Tun.
HADLEY WOOD
EPPING
INGATESTONE
WOODHAM FERRERS
Watford Tun.
GARSTON
Hadley N.Tun.
GORDON HILL
WALTHAM CROSS
THEYDON BOIS

G

CHORLEYWOOD
WATFORD NORTH
WATFORD JUNC.
Hadley S.Tun.
ELSTREE
HIGH BARNET
ENFIELD LOCK
BRIMSDOWN
DEBDEN
LOUGHTON
RICKMANS-WORTH
BUSHEY
Elstree Tun.
TOTTERIDGE
NEW BARNET
GRANGE PARK
PONDER'S END
CHINGFORD
SHENFIELD
Summit
BILLERICAY
BATTLESBRIDGE

5   4   Eighteen   3   2   1

A
B
C
D
E
F
G

SPOONER ROW
ATTLEBOROUGH
ECCLES ROAD
HARLING ROAD
THETFORD

HADDISCOE
SOMERLEYTON
OULTON BROAD NORTH
LOWESTOFT
BECCLES
OULTON BROAD SOUTH
Swing Bridge

BRAMPTON
HALESWORTH
DARSHAM

DISS

THURSTON
BURY ST. EDMUNDS
ELMSWELL
Haughley Jc.
STOWMARKET
NEEDHAM MARKET

SAXMUNDHAM
SIZEWELL
WICKHAM MARKET

MELTON
WESTERFIELD
WOODBRIDGE
East Suffolk Jc.
DERBY ROAD
LOWER YARD
GRIFFEN WHARF
IPSWICH

SUDBURY
BURES

TRIMLEY
FELIXSTOWE
DOCKS

MANNINGTREE
North Jc.
East Jc.
MISTLEY
WRABNESS
HARWICH TOWN
HARWICH INTERNATIONAL
DOVERCOURT

CHAPPEL & WAKES COLNE
COLCHESTER
COLCHESTER TOWN
MARKS TEY
Hythe Jc.
HYTHE
WIVENHOE
ALRESFORD
GREAT BENTLEY
WEELEY
KIRBY CROSS
WALTON-ON-NAZE
THORPE-LE-SOKEN
FRINTON

KELVEDON
WITHAM
CLACTON

FAMBRIDGE
ALTHORNE
SOUTHMINSTER
BURNHAM ON CROUCH

1   2   3   4   5

BIRMINGHAM DISTRICT
(INSET ON SHEET No. FIFTEEN)

A

PRIESTFIELD
THE CRESCENT
Darlaston Jc.
Pleck Jc.
BILSTON CENTRAL
East Jc.
LOXDALE
BRADLEY LANE
COSELEY
WEDNESBURY
PARKWAY
Goods Branch Jc.
WEDNESBURY GREAT
WESTERN STREET
South Jc.
BESCOT STADIUM
TAME BRIDGE
PARKWAY
HAMSTEAD

DYFFRYN ARDUDWY
TALYBONT
LLANABER
Barmouth
Bridge
BARMOUTH
MORFA MAWDDACH
FAIRBOURNE
Cader
Idris
LLWYNGWRIL

B

TIPTON
Line disused
Hill Top
Tunnel
BLACK LAKE
DUDLEY ST/
GUNS VILLAGE
LODGE ROAD
WEST BROMWICH
TOWN HALL
WEST BROMWICH CENTRAL
DARTMOUTH
STREET
Perry Barr
North Jc.
Perry Barr West Jc
PERRY
BARR
GRAVELLY HILL
WITTON
DUDLEY PORT
DUDLEY
TRINITY WAY
KENRICK PARK
Handsworth Jc.
SANDWELL &
DUDLEY
THE HAWTHORNS
SMETHWICK
GALTON BRIDGE
HANDSWORTH
BOOTH ST.
Soho Pool Jc.
ASTON

ABERGYNOLWYN
DOLGOCH FALLS
TONFANAU
Talyllyn
BRYNGLAS
RHYDYRONEN
PENDRE
WHARF STA.
TYWYN
ABERDOVEY
PENHELIG

C

LANGLEY GREEN
Galton Jc.
SMETHWICK
ROLFE ST
WINSON GREEN
OUTER CIRCLE
Soho East Jc.
SOHO BENSON ROAD
DUDDESTON
JEWELLERY QUARTER
Hockley Tunnel
SNOW
HILL
ST PAULS
Landor Street Jc.
LAWLEY STR.
ADDERLEY PARK
New Street
North Tunnel
NEW
ST.
Curzon
Str.Jc.
St. Andrew's Jc.
FIVE WAYS
MOOR ST.
BORDESLEY
Bordesley
Jc.
UNIVERSITY

BORTH

ABERYSTWYTH
GLANRAFON
LLANBADARN
Vale of
Rheidol
CAPEL
BANGOR

OLD HILL
ROWLEY REGIS
Old Hill Tunnel

D

E

F

FOREST
HALT
PONTPRENSHITW
LLANDYFRIOG
HENLLAN
Teifi Valley
Railway

FISHGUARD
HARBOUR

Letterston Jc.
TRECWN

G

CYNWYL ELFED (proposed)
Gwili Railway
DANYCOED
LLWYFAN
CERRIG
BRONWYDD ARMS
LLANDEILO

Spittal Tun.
CLARBESTON ROAD
Clarbeston Jc.
CLUNDERWEN
WHITLAND
Carmarthen
Bridge Jc.
CARMARTHEN
Carmarthen Jc.
FFAIRFACH

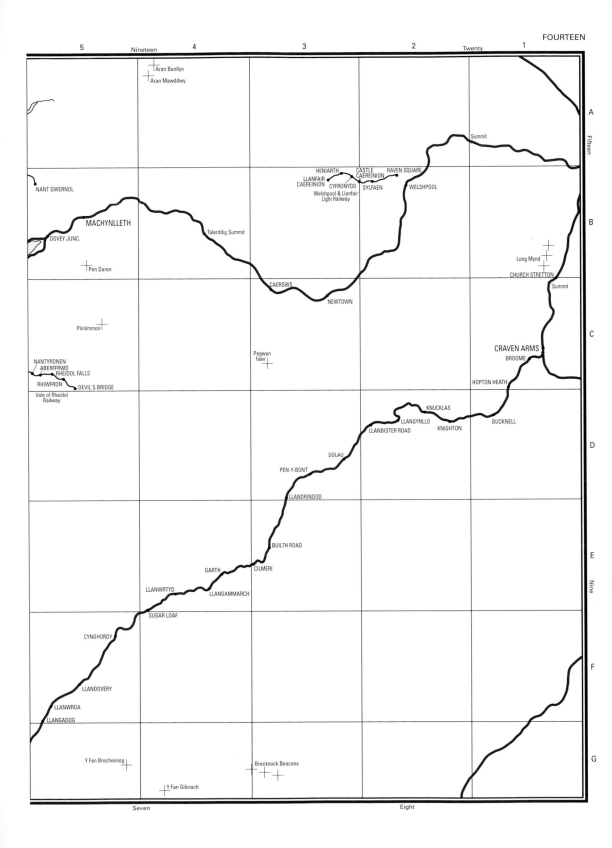

1   2   Twenty   3   4   Twenty one   5

(SEE SHEET NO.FORTY FIVE)

Column A area:
HOUGH GN
WIDNES
HALEWOOD
ICI WORKS
INCE & ELTON
HELSBY
FRODSHAM
Frodsham Jc.
Halton Jc.
RUNCORN
Sutton Tun.
TANHOUSE LANE
RUNCORN EAST
Acton Grange Jc.
FIDDLER'S FERRY
WARRINGTON
LATCHFORD
ALTRINCHAM
HALE
HEALD GREEN
CHEADLE HULME
WOODSMOOR
DAVENPORT
HAZEL GROVE
STRINES
NEW MILLS CENTRAL
NEW MILLS NEWTOWN
Disley Tunnel
MIDDLEWOOD
BRAMHALL
POYNTON
ASHLEY
MANCHESTER AIRPORT
STYAL
HANDFORTH
MOBBERLEY
WILMSLOW
ADLINGTON
DISLEY
FURNESS VALE
WHALEY BRIDGE
N.Jc.
CHINLEY
Chinley E.Jc.
Cowburn Tun.
EDALE
HOPE
BAMFORD
HATHERSAGE
KNUTSFORD
WEAVER Jc.
WINNINGTON
PLUMLEY
ALDERLEY EDGE
Prestbury Tun.
PRESTBURY
CHAPEL-EN-LE-FRITH
DOVE HOLES
Dove Holes Tun.
Summit
PEAK FOREST
MOULDSWORTH
CUDDINGTON
ACTON BRIDGE
GREENBANK
NORTHWICH
LOSTOCK GRALAM
CHELFORD
Hibel Rd Tunnel
MACCLESFIELD
BUXTON
Mickle Trafford Jc.
DELAMERE
HARTFORD
GOOSTREY
Summit
HINDLOW
Christleton Tun.
WINSFORD
HOLMES CHAPEL
SANDBACH
CONGLETON
PREES
WEM
YORTON
WHITCHURCH
Summit
WRENBURY
NANTWICH
Crewe North Jc.
Manchester Line Jc.
Gresty Lane Jc.
N.S. Jc.
CREWE
Basford Hall Jc.
ALSAGER
KIDSGROVE
Harecastle Tun.
LONGPORT
Leek Brook Jc.
Cheddleton Tun.
CHEDDLETON
Churnet Valley Railway
CONSALL
CALDON LOW
KINGSLEY & FROGHALL
STOKE
LONGTON
Meir Tunnel
BLYTHE BRIDGE
WEDGWOOD
BARLASTON
STONE
Summit
NORTON BRIDGE
UTTOXETER
BURTON-ON-TRENT
TUTBURY & HATTON
BURTON-ON-TRENT
(SEE INSET)
Leicester Jc.
Branston Jc.
Birmingham Curve Jc.
STAFFORD
Trent Valley Jc.
Colwich Jc.
Shugborough Tun.
RUGELEY (T.V.)
RUGELEY TOWN
Wichnor Jc.
Bushbury Jc.
WOLVERHAMPTON ST GEORGES
WOLVERHAMPTON Crane St. Jc.
THE ROYAL
Heath Town Jc.
PENKRIDGE
HEDNESFORD
CANNOCK
LICHFIELD
TRENT VALLEY
CITY
SHREWSBURY
English Bridge Jc.
Abbey Foregate Jc.
Sutton Bridge Jc.
WELLINGTON
The Wrekin
OAKENGATES
TELFORD CENTRAL
Madeley Jc.
SHIFNAL
COSFORD
ALBRIGHTON
CODSALL
BILBROOK
PRIESTFIELD
LANDYWOOD
BLOXWICH NORTH
BLOXWICH
Bushbury Jc.
BROWNHILLS
SHENSTONE
TAMWORTH
WILNECOTE
BADDESLEY
IRONBRIDGE POWER STATION
Caer Caradoc
CHURCH STRETTON
BRIDGNORTH
(SEE INSET ON SHEET NO THIRTEEN)
WOLVERHAMPTON
BLAKE STR.
BUTLERS LANE
FOUR OAKS
SUTTON COLDFIELD
Kingsbury Jc.
Whitacre Jc.
Ryecroft Jc.
WALSALL
BESCOT STADIUM
TAME BRIDGE PARKWAY
HAMSTEAD
PERRY BARR
WYLDE GREEN
CHESTER RD
WATER ORTON
ERDINGTON
Brown Clee
Severn Valley Railway
HAMPTON LOADE
COUNTRY PARK HALT
HIGHLEY
SHUT END
ROUND OAK
CRADLEY HEATH
LANGLEY GREEN
ROWLEY REGIS
OLD HILL
GRAVELLY HILL
ASTON
SNOW HILL
FIVE WAYS
UNIVERSITY
NEW STREET
SELLY OAK
BIRMINGHAM
ADDERLEY PARK
STECHFORD
LEA HALL
MARSTON GREEN
BIRMINGHAM INTERNATIONAL
HAMPTON-IN-ARDEN
BORDESLEY
SMALLHEATH
TYSELY
ACOCKS GREEN
OLTON
HALL GREEN
SPRING ROAD
BOURNVILLE
STOURBRIDGE TOWN
STOURBRIDGE JC.
LYE
Nine

Fourteen
Twenty

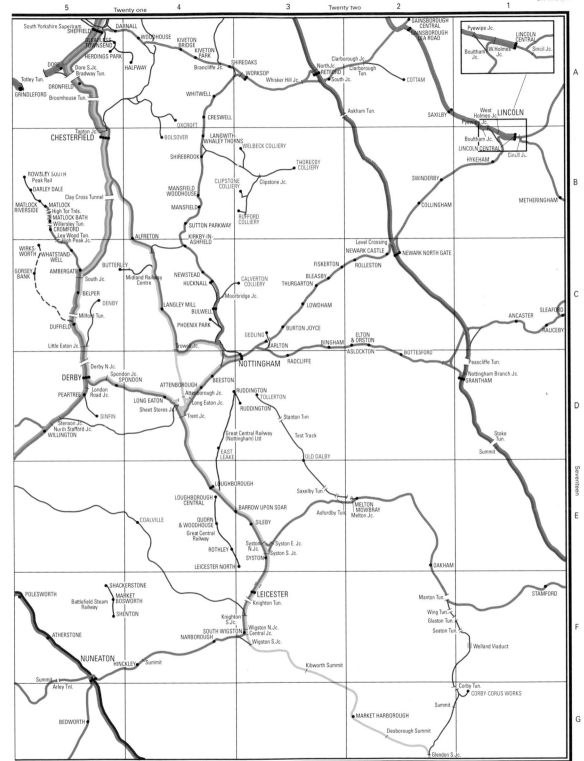

South Yorkshire Supertram
SHEFFIELD
GLEADLESS
TOWNSEND
DARNALL
WOODHOUSE
KIVETON BRIDGE
KIVETON PARK
SHIREOAKS
HERDINGS PARK
HALFWAY
Brancliffe Jc.
WORKSOP
Whisker Hill Jc.
Clarborough Jc.
North Jc.
RETFORD
South Jc.
Clarborough Tun.
GAINSBOROUGH CENTRAL
GAINSBOROUGH LEA ROAD
Pyewipe Jc.
W.Holmes Jc.
LINCOLN CENTRAL
Boultham Jc.
Sincil Jc.
A
DORE
Totley Tun.
DRONFIELD
Dore S.Jc.
Bradway Tun.
WHITWELL
COTTAM
GRINDLEFORD
Broomhouse Tun.
CRESWELL
Askham Tun.
SAXILBY
West Holmes Jc.
LINCOLN
Pyewipe Jc.
CHESTERFIELD
Tapton Jc.
OXCROFT
BOLSOVER
LANGWITH-
WHALEY THORNS
WELBECK COLLIERY
Boultham Jc.
LINCOLN CENTRAL
Sincil Jc.
SHIREBROOK
THORESBY COLLIERY
HYKEHAM
B
ROWSLEY SOUTH
Peak Rail
DARLEY DALE
Clay Cross Tunnel
MATLOCK
High Tor Tnls.
MATLOCK
RIVERSIDE
MATLOCK BATH
Willersley Tun.
CROMFORD
Lea Wood Tun.
High Peak Jc.
WIRKS-
WORTH
WHATSTAND-
WELL
GORSEY
BANK
AMBERGATE
BUTTERLEY
South Jc.
Midland Railway
Centre
BELPER
DENBY
DUFFIELD
Milford Tun.
Little Eaton Jc.
MANSFIELD
WOODHOUSE
MANSFIELD
SUTTON PARKWAY
KIRKBY-IN-
ASHFIELD
ALFRETON
NEWSTEAD
HUCKNALL
Moorbridge Jc.
LANGLEY MILL
BULWELL
PHOENIX PARK
CLIPSTONE
COLLIERY
Clipstone Jc.
RUFFORD
COLLIERY
CALVERTON
COLLIERY
SWINDERBY
COLLINGHAM
METHERINGHAM
Level Crossing
NEWARK CASTLE
FISKERTON
ROLLESTON
BLEASBY
THURGARTON
NEWARK NORTH GATE
ANCASTER
SLEAFORD
RAUCEBY
C
GEDLING
CARLTON
BURTON JOYCE
LOWDHAM
BINGHAM
ELTON
& ORSTON
ASLOCKTON
BOTTESFORD
Trowell Jc.
NOTTINGHAM
RADCLIFFE
Peascliffe Tun.
Nottingham Branch Jc.
GRANTHAM
D
DERBY
Derby N Jc.
Spondon Jc.
SPONDON
PEARTREE
London
Road Jc.
SINFIN
ATTENBOROUGH
Attenborough Jc.
LONG EATON
Sheet Stores Jc.
BEESTON
Long Eaton Jc.
Trent Jc.
RUDDINGTON
TOLLERTON
RUDDINGTON
Stanton Tun.
Stenson Jc.
North Stafford Jc.
WILLINGTON
Great Central Railway
(Nottingham) Ltd
EAST
LEAKE
Test Track
OLD DALBY
Stoke
Tun.
Summit
E
LOUGHBOROUGH
LOUGHBOROUGH
CENTRAL
BARROW UPON SOAR
Saxelby Tun.
MELTON
MOWBRAY
Melton Jc.
Asfordby Tun.
COALVILLE
QUORN
& WOODHOUSE
Great Central
Railway
ROTHLEY
SILEBY
Syston
N.Jc.
Syston E. Jc.
Syston S. Jc.
SYSTON
OAKHAM
LEICESTER NORTH
SHACKERSTONE
MARKET
BOSWORTH
Battlefield Steam
Railway
SHENTON
LEICESTER
Knighton Tun.
Manton Tun.
STAMFORD
POLESWORTH
Wing Tun.
Glaston Tun.
Knighton
S.Jc.
Seaton Tun.
ATHERSTONE
Wigston N.Jc.
SOUTH WIGSTON
Central Jc.
NARBOROUGH
Wigston S.Jc.
Welland Viaduct
F
NUNEATON
HINCKLEY
Summit
Kibworth Summit
Corby Tun.
CORBY-CORUS WORKS
Summit
Arley Tnl.
BEDWORTH
MARKET HARBOROUGH
Summit
Desborough Summit
Glendon S.Jc.
G

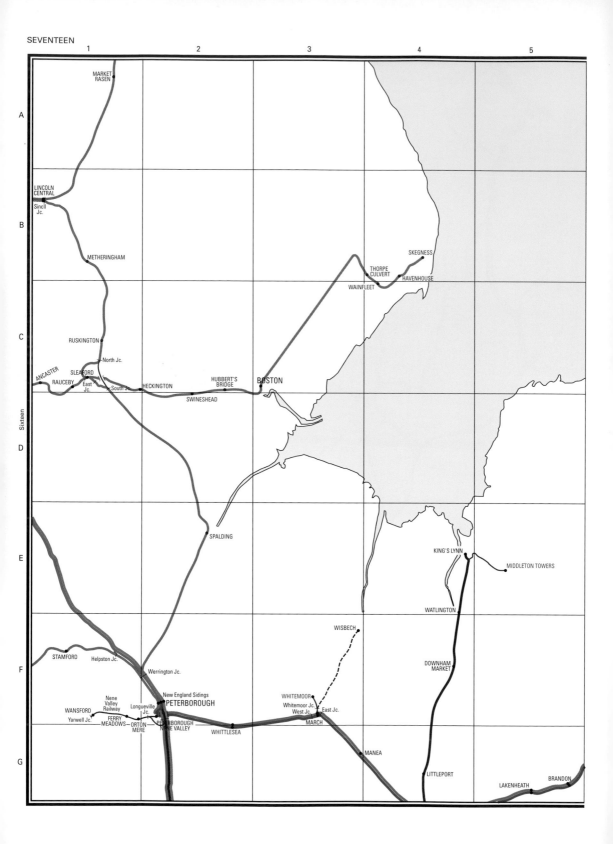

1   2   3   4   5

A

B

C

D

E

F

G

Sixteen

MARKET RASEN

LINCOLN CENTRAL
Sincll Jc.

METHERINGHAM

RUSKINGTON

SKEGNESS
THORPE CULVERT
HAVENHOUSE
WAINFLEET

ANCASTER
RAUCEBY
SLEAFORD
North Jc.
East Jc.
South Jc.
HECKINGTON
SWINESHEAD
HUBBERT'S BRIDGE
BOSTON

SPALDING

KING'S LYNN
MIDDLETON TOWERS

WATLINGTON

WISBECH

STAMFORD
Helpston Jc.
Werrington Jc.

DOWNHAM MARKET

Nene Valley Railway
New England Sidings
WANSFORD
Yarwell Jc.
FERRY MEADOWS
Longueville Jc.
ORTON MERE
PETERBOROUGH
PETERBOROUGH NENE VALLEY
WHITTLESEA
WHITEMOOR
Whitemoor Jc.
West Jc.
East Jc.
MARCH

MANEA

LITTLEPORT
LAKENHEATH
BRANDON

5   4   3   2   1

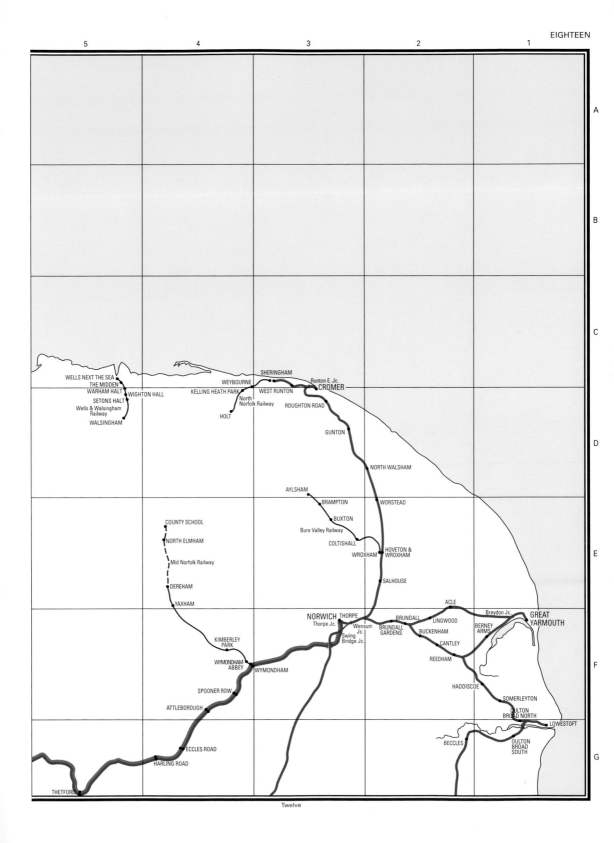

A

B

C

WELLS NEXT THE SEA
THE MIDDEN
WARHAM HALT   WIGHTON HALL
SETONS HALT
Wells & Walsingham
Railway
WALSINGHAM

SHERINGHAM
WEYBOURNE
KELLING HEATH PARK   WEST RUNTON   Runton E. Jc.
North   CROMER
Norfolk Railway   ROUGHTON ROAD
HOLT

GUNTON

NORTH WALSHAM

D

AYLSHAM
BRAMPTON   WORSTEAD
BUXTON
COUNTY SCHOOL   Bure Valley Railway
NORTH ELMHAM   COLTISHALL   HOVETON &
WROXHAM   WROXHAM
Mid Norfolk Railway
SALHOUSE
DEREHAM
YAXHAM

E

ACLE   Breydon Jc.
NORWICH   THORPE   GREAT
Thorpe Jc.   BRUNDALL   LINGWOOD   YARMOUTH
Wensum   BRUNDALL   BERNEY
KIMBERLEY   Jc.   GARDENS   BUCKENHAM   ARMS
PARK   Swing   CANTLEY
Bridge Jc.
WYMONDHAM   REEDHAM
ABBEY   WYMONDHAM
SPOONER ROW   HADDISCOE
SOMERLEYTON
ATTLEBOROUGH   OULTON
BROAD NORTH   LOWESTOFT

F

ECCLES ROAD   BECCLES   OULTON
HARLING ROAD   BROAD
SOUTH

THETFORD

G

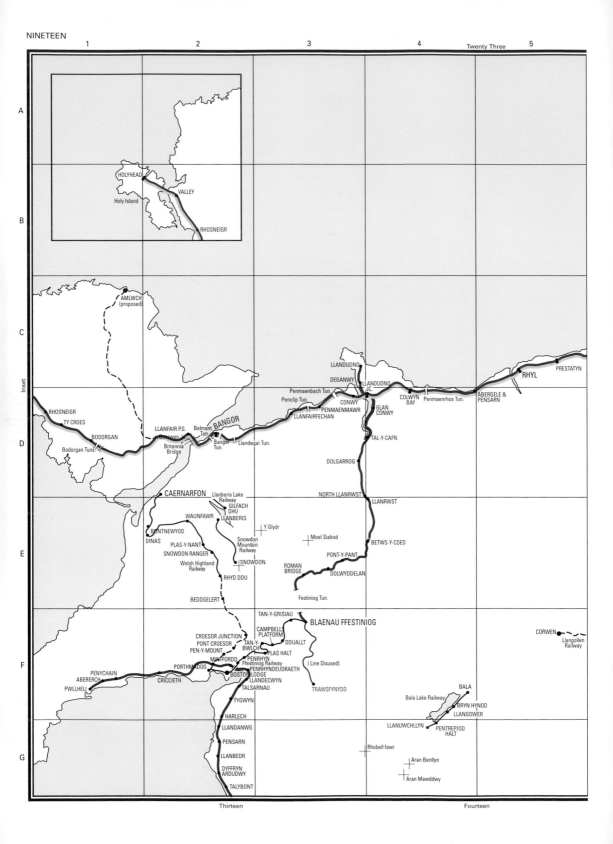

1   2   3   4   Twenty Three   5

A

HOLYHEAD
VALLEY
Holy Island
RHOSNEIGR

B

AMLWCH
(proposed)

Inset

LLANDUDNO
DEGANWY
LLANDUDNO
JC.
Penmaenbach Tun.
Penclip Tun.
RHYL   PRESTATYN
CONWY
GLAN
CONWY
PENMAENMAWR
COLWYN
BAY   Penmaenrhos Tun.   ABERGELE &
PENSARN
LLANFAIRFECHAN

RHOSNEIGR
TY CROES
BODORGAN
Bodorgan Tuns.
LLANFAIR P.G.
Belmont
Tun.
BANGOR
Gaerwen Jc.
Britannia
Bridge
Bangor
Tun.
Llandegai Tun.
TAL-Y-CAFN

D

DOLGARROG

CAERNARFON
Llanberis Lake
Railway
GILFACH
DHU
LLANBERIS
WAUNFAWR
NORTH LLANRWST
LLANRWST

E

BONTNEWYDD
DINAS
PLAS-Y-NANT
SNOWDON RANGER
Welsh Highland
Railway
RHYD DDU
Y Glydr
Snowdon
Mountain
Railway
SNOWDON
Moel Siabod
ROMAN
BRIDGE
Festiniog Tun.
PONT-Y-PANT
DOLWYDDELAN
BETWS-Y-COED

BEDDGELERT

TAN-Y-GRISIAU
CAMPBELL'S
PLATFORM
DDUALLT
BLAENAU FFESTINIOG
CORWEN
Llangollen
Railway

F

CROESOR JUNCTION
PONT CROESOR
PEN-Y-MOUNT
TAN-Y-
BWLCH
PLAS HALT
MINFFORDD
PENRHYN
Ffestiniog Railway
PORTHMADOG
BOSTON LODGE
PENRHYNDEUDRAETH
(Line Disused)
PENYCHAIN
ABERERCH
CRICCIETH
LLANDECWYN
TALSARNAU
TRAWSFYNYDD
BALA
Bala Lake Railway
BRYN HYNOD
LLANGOWER
PWLLHELI
TYGWYN
HARLECH
LLANDANWG
LLANUWCHLLYN
PENTREPIOD
HALT
PENSARN
LLANBEDR
Rhobell fawr
DYFFRYN
ARDUDWY
Aran Benllyn
TALYBONT
Aran Mawddwy

G

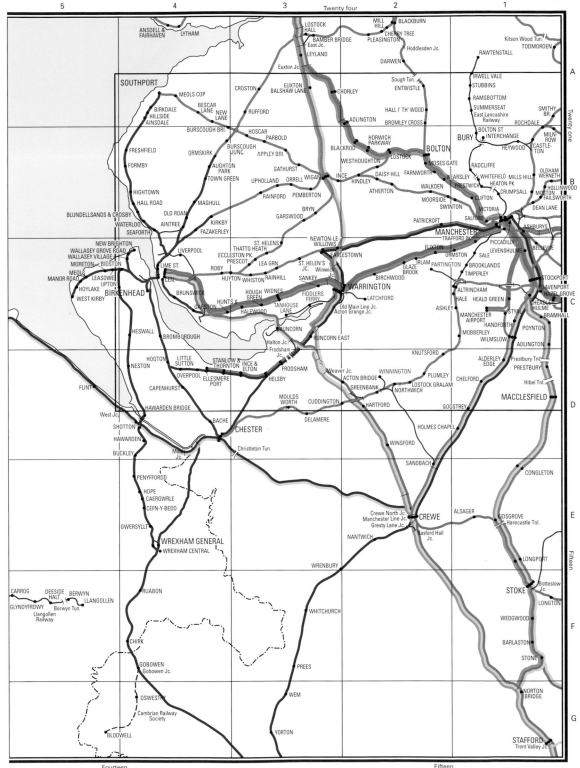

5   4   3   Twenty four   2   1

ANSDELL &
FAIRHAVEN   LYTHAM

LOSTOCK
HALL
BAMBER BRIDGE
East Jc.
LEYLAND

Euxton Jc.

MILL
HILL   BLACKBURN
CHERRY TREE
PLEASINGTON

Hoddlesden Jc.

DARWEN

Kitson Wood Tun.   TODMORDEN

RAWTENSTALL

SOUTHPORT

MEOLS COP

BIRKDALE
HILLSIDE
AINSDALE

BESCAR
LANE
NEW
LANE

BURSCOUGH BRI.

FRESHFIELD

FORMBY

ORMSKIRK

AUGHTON
PARK
TOWN GREEN

HIGHTOWN

HALL ROAD

MAGHULL

BLUNDELLSANDS & CROSBY
WATERLOO
SEAFORTH

CROSTON

RUFFORD

EUXTON
BALSHAW LANE

HOSCAR

PARBOLD

BURSCOUGH
JUNC.
APPLEY DRI.

UPHOLLAND

RAINFORD

GATHURST

ORRELL   WIGAN
INCE
HINDLEY

PEMBERTON

BRYN

GARSWOOD

CHORLEY

ADLINGTON

HALL I' TH' WOOD

BROMLEY CROSS

BLACKROD

WESTHOUGHTON

DAISY HILL

ATHERTON

Sough Tun.
ENTWISTLE

HORWICH
PARKWAY

LOSTOCK

BOLTON

MOSES GATE

FARNWORTH

WALKDEN

MOORSIDE

SWINTON

IRWELL VALE
STUBBINS
RAMSBOTTOM
SUMMERSEAT
East Lancashire
Railway

BURY

HEYWOOD

RADCLIFFE

KEARSLEY   WHITEFIELD
PRESTWICH

CLIFTON

SMITHY
BR.
ROCHDALE

MILN-
ROW

BOLTON ST
INTERCHANGE
MILLS HILL

HEATON PK
CRUMPSALL

VICTORIA

CASTLE-
TON

OLDHAM
WERNETH
HOLLINWOOD
MOSTON
FAILSWORTH
DEAN LANE

NEW BRIGHTON
WALLASEY GROVE ROAD
WALLASEY VILLAGE
MORETON   BIDSTON
MEOLS
MANOR ROAD
HOYLAKE
WEST KIRBY
BIRKENHEAD

LEASOWE
UPTON

LIVERPOOL
LIME ST.
CEN.

BRUNSWICK

GARSTON

ST. HELENS
THATTO HEATH
ECCLESTON PK.
PRESCOT
LEA GRN.
ROBY
RAINHILL
HUYTON   WHISTON

HOUGH
GREEN   WIDNES
HUNTS X

TANHOUSE
HALEWOOD   LANE

NEWTON-LE-
WILLOWS   EARLESTOWN

ST. HELEN'S
JC.   Winwick
SANKEY   Jc.

FIDDLERS
FERRY

BIRCHWOOD

WARRINGTON
LATCHFORD
Old Main Line Jc.
Acton Grange Jc.

FLIXTON

URMSTON
IRLAM   PARTINGTON
GLAZE
BROOK

PATRICROFT   SALFORD

TRAFFORD PK

MANCHESTER
PICCADILLY
LEVENSHULME
SALE   BROOKLANDS
TIMPERLEY

ASHBURYS
BELLEVUE

STOCKPORT
DAVENPORT
HAZEL GROVE

HEATON
ALTRINCHAM   HEALD GREEN   CHAPEL
HALE   MANCHESTER
ASHLEY   AIRPORT
HANDFORTH
MOBBERLEY

STYAL

CHEADLE
HULME
BRAMHALL

POYNTON

WILMSLOW

ADLINGTON

HESWALL

BROMBOROUGH

HOOTON
NESTON

LITTLE
SUTTON
OVERPOOL

CAPENHURST

FLINT

HAWARDEN BRIDGE

STANLOW &
THORNTON   INCE &
ELTON
ELLESMERE
PORT   FRODSHAM
HELSBY

Halton Jc.
Frodsham
Jc.

RUNCORN

RUNCORN EAST

Weaver Jc.
ACTON BRIDGE
GREENBANK

KNUTSFORD

WINNINGTON
PLUMLEY
LOSTOCK GRALAM
NORTHWICH

ALDERLEY
EDGE   Prestbury Tnl.
PRESTBURY

CHELFORD   Hibel Tnl.

MACCLESFIELD

West Jc.

SHOTTON

HAWARDEN

BUCKLEY

BACHE

Mold
Jc.

CHESTER

Christleton Tun.

MOULDS
WORTH   CUDDINGTON

DELAMERE

HARTFORD

WINSFORD

GOOSTREY

HOLMES CHAPEL

SANDBACH

CONGLETON

PENYFFORDD

HOPE
CAERGWRLE
CEFN-Y-BEDD

GWERSYLLT

WREXHAM GENERAL
WREXHAM CENTRAL

CREWE NORTH Jc.
Manchester Line Jc.
Gresty Lane Jc.

NANTWICH

WRENBURY

CREWE

Basford Hall
Jc.

ALSAGER   KIDSGROVE
Harecastle Tnl.

LONGPORT

STOKE

Botteslow
Jc.
LONGTON

CARROG   DEESIDE
HALT   BERWYN
LLANGOLLEN
GLYNDYFRDWY   Berwyn Tun.
Llangollen
Railway

RUABON

CHIRK

GOBOWEN
Gobowen Jc.

OSWESTRY

Cambrian Railway
Society

BLODWELL

WHITCHURCH

PREES

WEM

YORTON

WEDGWOOD

BARLASTON

STONE

NORTON
BRIDGE

STAFFORD
Trent Valley Jc.

A

B

C

D

E

F

G

Twenty one

Fifteen

Fourteen   Fifteen

REDMIRE

NORTHALLERTON
South J.c.

Skelton Jc.

Severus Jc.

North Jc.

YORK

Holgate Bridge

THIRSK

Ashton Moss
North Jc.
ASHTON-UNDER-LYME

STALYBRIDGE

GUIDE BRIDGE

Denton Jc.

COLNE
NELSON

RYLSTONE

GARGRAVE

Wortley Jc.
LEEDS

Canal Jc.
Leeds Jc.
Engine
Shed Jc.

Wortley S. Jc.

N.

STARBECK
KNARESBOROUGH
CATTAL
HAMMERTON

HARROGATE
HORNBEAM
PARK
PANNAL

POPPLETON
Skelton Jc.
Severus Jc.
YORK
Bootham Jc.
Burton Lane Jc.

Holgate Bridge Jc.

EMBSAY

Skipton
N. Jc.
SKIPTON

HOLYWELL
HALT

BOLTON ABBEY
Embsay & Bolton Abbey
Steam Railway

WEETON

GARGRAVE

CONONLEY

STEETON
& SILSDEN
ILKLEY

BEN RHYDDING
BURLEY in WHARFEDALE

MENSTON
GUISELEY

Bramhope Tun.

ULLESKELF

Colton Junction

Worth Valley Bch Jc.
West
INGROW WEST
DAMEMS
OAKWORTH
HAWORTH

OXENHOPE
Keighley & Worth
Valley Railway

KEIGHLEY
CROSSFLATTS
BINGLEY
BAILDON
Bingley Tun.
SALTAIRE
SHIPLEY

FRIZINGHALL

BRADFORD

HORSFORTH

BRAMLEY
NEW
PUDSEY

LEEDS

Bowling Tun.

COTTINGLEY

MORLEY

CROSS
GATES
GARFORTH

EAST
GARFORTH

Hunslet Bch Jc.

MICKLEFIELD

SOUTH
MILFORD
Milford Jc.

CHURCH
FENTON

SHERBURN-IN-ELMET
Gasgoigne
Wood Jc.
Swing Bri.
E. Jc.

SELBY
Brayton N. Jc.
WRESSLE

WOODLESFORD

Kitson
Wood
Tun.
Hall Royd Jc.
Millwood Tun.

Horsfall Tun.
Castle Hill Tun.

TODMORDEN
WALSDEN
Winterbutlee Tun.
Summit
Tun.

Weasel Hall Tun.
HEBDEN BRI.
MYTHOLMROYD

SOWERBY BRI.

Wyke Tun.

HALIFAX
Bank House Tun.

BRIGHOUSE

Bradley
Wood Jc.
MIRFIELD

Morley
Tun.
BATLEY

DEWSBURY
RAVENSTHORPE

L.N.W. Jc.

NORMANTON

CASTLEFORD

GLASS
HOUGHTON
TANSHELF
STREETHOUSE
FEATHERSTONE

PONTEFRACT
MONKHILL
KNOTTINGLEY

PONTEFRACT BAGHILL

Temple Hirst Jc.

WHITLEY
BRIDGE
HENSALL

DRAX

SNAITH
RAWCLIFFE

THORNE NORTH

LITTLEBOROUGH

SMITHY BRIDGE

Rochdale E. Jc.
ROCHDALE
MILNROW
NEW HEY
SHAW &
CROMPTON

DEIGHTON

HUDDERSFIELD

LOCKWOOD
BERRY BROW
Robin Hood Tun.

MARSDEN
Standedge Tun.

SLAITHWAITE

HONLEY
STOCKS-
MOOR
SHEPLEY

BROCKHOLES
Thurstonland Tun.

SHELLEY
DENBY DALE

CUCKOO'S
NEST

Steeple Grange
Light Railway
CLAYTON WEST

SKELMANTHORPE
Cumberworth Tun.

DARTON

MONK
BRETTON

WAKE-
FIELD

Brackenhill Jc.

FITZWILLIAM

Shafton Jc.
MOORTHORPE

Shaftholme Jc.

Joan Croft Jc. Thorne Jc.
Applehurst Jc.

THORNE
SOUTH

HATFIELD &
STAINFORTH

OLDHAM
MUMPS
OLDHAM
DERKER

OLDHAM
WERNETH

GREENFIELD

MOSSLEY

Scout Tunnel

WELLHOUSE Jc.
PENISTONE

SILKSTONE
COMMON

BARNSLEY

WOMBWELL

ELSECAR
Tankersley Tun.

SWINTON

THURNSCOE
Hickleton
S. Jc.

GOLDTHORPE
BOLTON ON
DEANE

MEXBORO

CONISBOROUGH

Adwick Jc.
Skellow Jc.
ADWICK

Castle Hills Jc.

BENTLEY

KIRK SANDALL

Kirk Sandall Jc.
Bentley Jc.

DONCASTER

South Yorkshire Jc.
Blackcarr Jc.
Bessacar Jc.

St Catherine's
Jcs.
Loversall
Carr Jc.

ASHTON

STALYBRIDGE

GUIDE BRIDGE

DENTON
Denton
Jc.

HYDE NORTH
1 3 4 5
HYDE CENTRAL DINTING

HADFIELD

GLOSSOP

Reddish
Jc.
WOODLEY

BREDBURY
ROMILEY

DAVEN-
PORT
ROSE
HILL
MARPLE
STRINES

WOODSMOOR

HAZEL GROVE

BENTLEY

Kirk
Sandall Jc.
Bentley Jc.

N.Jc.
Belby Jc.
S.Jc.

Marshgate Jc.
DONCASTER
South Yorkshire Jc.

Potteric Carr Jc.
Low Ellers Jc.

Hexthorpe
Doncaster Avoiding Line Jc.

Black Carr Jc.

Bessaoar Jc.
Lowersall
Carr Jc.

Black Carr E. Jc.
St Catherine's Jcs.

STOCKSBRIDGE

CHAPELTOWN

MEADOWHALL

ROTHERHAM
CENTRAL
TINSLEY YARD

Tunnel Jc.

DARNALL
Treeton Jc.

SHEFFIELD

WOODHOUSE

HARWORTH

1 Flowery Field
2 Newton for Hyde
3 Godley

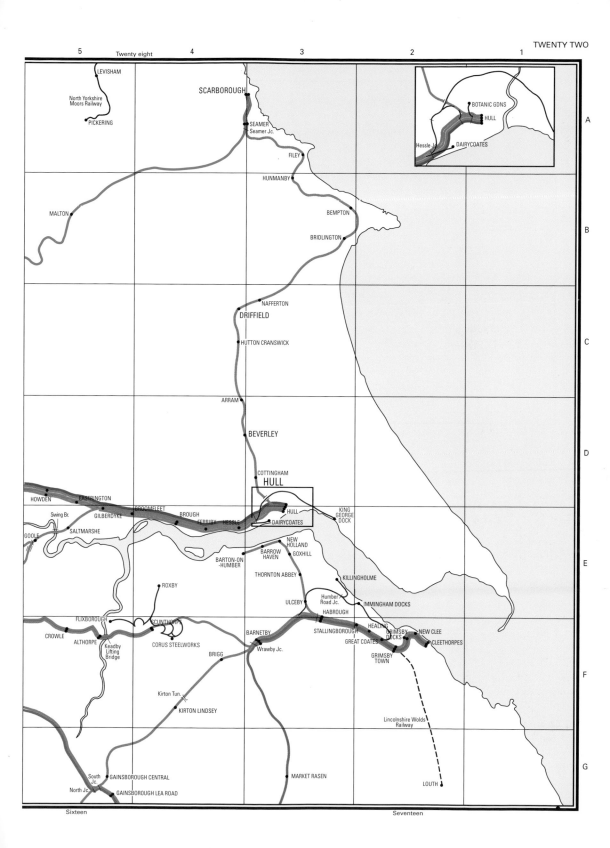

LEVISHAM

North Yorkshire
Moors Railway

PICKERING

SCARBOROUGH

SEAMER
Seamer Jc.

FILEY

HUNMANBY

MALTON

BEMPTON

BRIDLINGTON

BOTANIC GDNS
HULL

Hessle Jc.   DAIRYCOATES

NAFFERTON

DRIFFIELD

HUTTON CRANSWICK

ARRAM

BEVERLEY

COTTINGHAM
HULL

HOWDEN   EASTRINGTON
BROOMFLEET   BROUGH   HESSLE   HULL
Swing Br.   GILBERDYKE   FERRIBY   DAIRYCOATES   KING
GEORGE
DOCK
SALTMARSHE
GOOLE   NEW
HOLLAND
BARROW   GOXHILL
HAVEN
BARTON-ON
-HUMBER
THORNTON ABBEY   KILLINGHOLME

ROXBY   HUMBER
Road Jc.   IMMINGHAM DOCKS
ULCEBY
FLIXBOROUGH   SCUNTHORPE   HABROUGH
CROWLE   HEALING   GRIMSBY   NEW CLEE
ALTHORPE   BARNETBY   STALLINGBOROUGH   DOCKS
Keadby   CORUS STEELWORKS   GREAT COATES   CLEETHORPES
Lifting   Wrawby Jc.
Bridge   BRIGG   GRIMSBY
TOWN
Kirton Tun.
KIRTON LINDSEY

Lincolnshire Wolds
Railway

South   GAINSBOROUGH CENTRAL   MARKET RASEN
Jc.
North Jc.   GAINSBOROUGH LEA ROAD   LOUTH

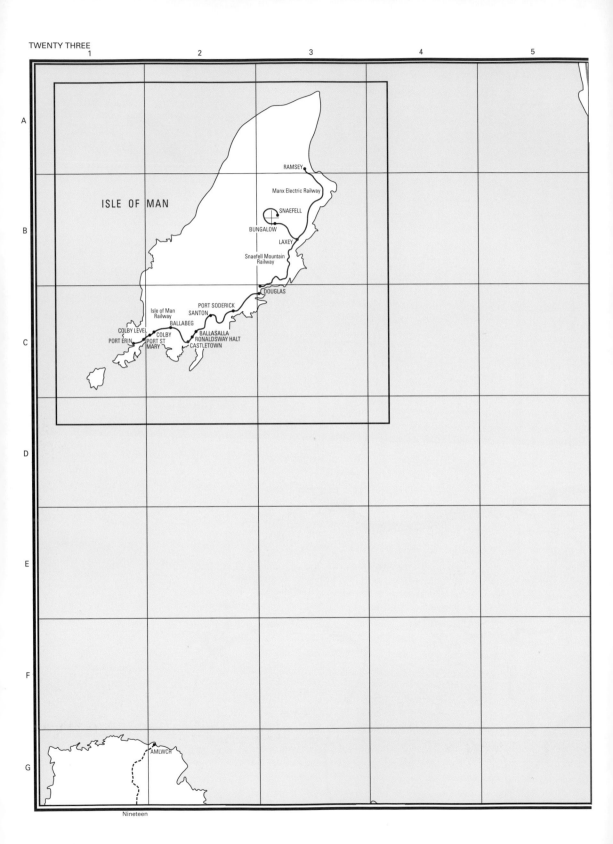

ISLE OF MAN

RAMSEY

Manx Electric Railway

SNAEFELL

BUNGALOW

LAXEY

Snaefell Mountain
Railway

DOUGLAS

PORT SODERICK

Isle of Man
Railway

SANTON

BALLABEG

COLBY LEVEL

BALLASALLA

COLBY

RONALDSWAY HALT

PORT ERIN

PORT ST
MARY

CASTLETOWN

AMLWCH

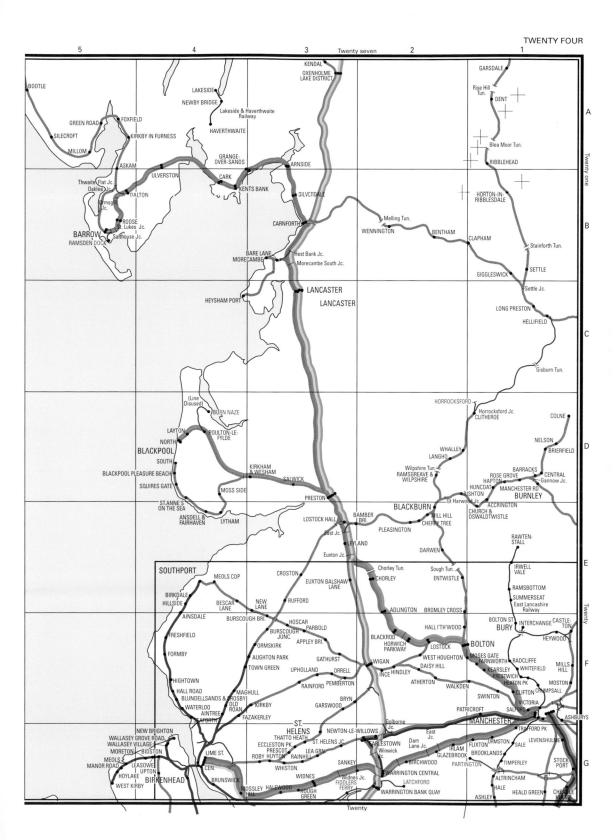

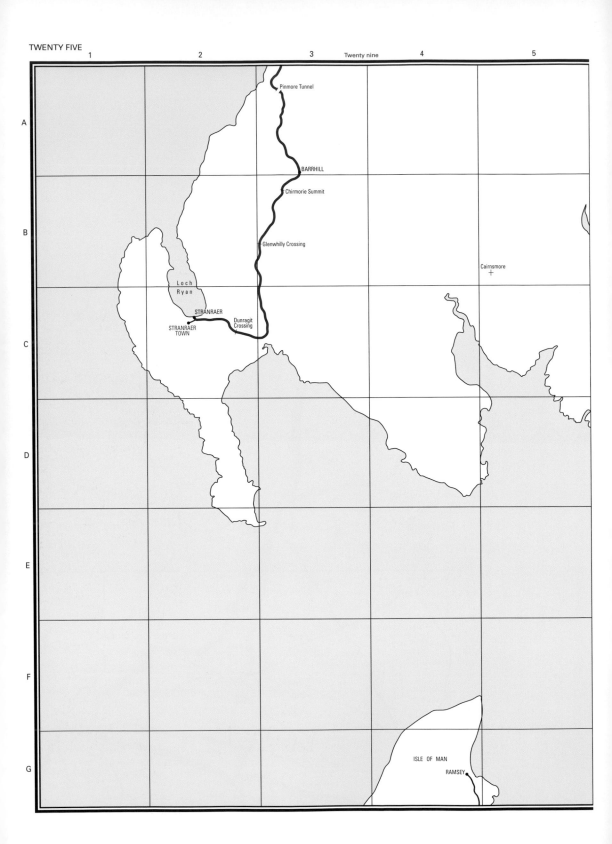

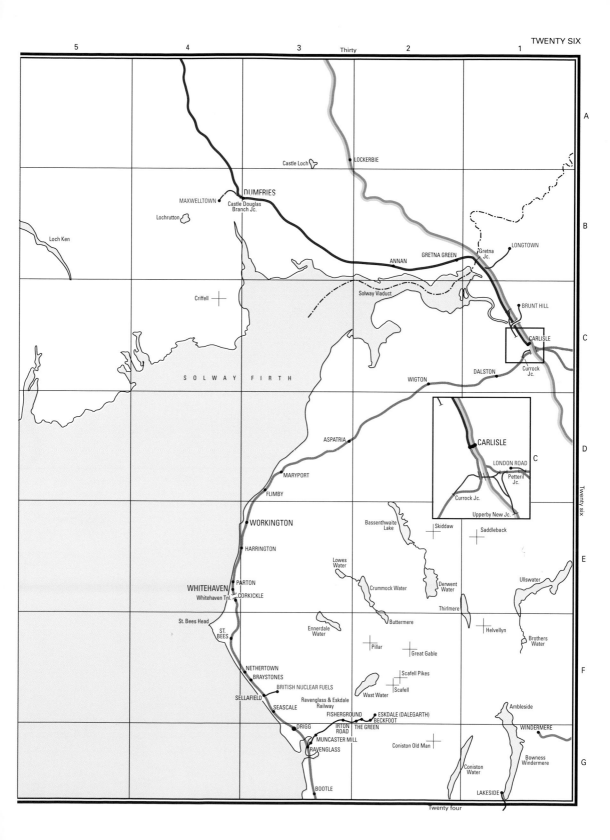

5   4   3   Thirty   2   1

A

Castle Loch

● LOCKERBIE

● MAXWELLTOWN ● DUMFRIES

Castle Douglas
Branch Jc.

Lochrutton

Loch Ken

B

ANNAN

GRETNA GREEN

Gretna
Jc.

● LONGTOWN

Criffell

Solway Viaduct

● BRUNT HILL

● CARLISLE

SOLWAY FIRTH

WIGTON

DALSTON

Currock
Jc.

C

ASPATRIA

CARLISLE

LONDON ROAD

Petteril
Jc.

Currock Jc.

C

MARYPORT

FLIMBY

Upperby New Jc.

Bassenthwaite
Lake

Skiddaw

Saddleback

D

Twenty six

● WORKINGTON

HARRINGTON

Lowes
Water

Crummock Water

Derwent
Water

Ullswater

E

PARTON

WHITEHAVEN ●

Whitehaven Tnl.
CORKICKLE

Thirlmere

St. Bees Head

ST.
BEES

Ennerdale
Water

Buttermere

Helvellyn

Brothers
Water

Pillar

Great Gable

F

NETHERTOWN

BRAYSTONES

BRITISH NUCLEAR FUELS

SELLAFIELD

SEASCALE

Ravenglass & Eskdale
Railway

FISHERGROUND

DRIGG

IRTON
ROAD

MUNCASTER MILL

RAVENGLASS

Wast Water

Scafell

Scafell Pikes

ESKDALE (DALEGARTH)

THE GREEN BECKFOOT

Coniston Old Man

Ambleside

● WINDERMERE

Bowness
Windermere

Coniston
Water

LAKESIDE

G

● BOOTLE

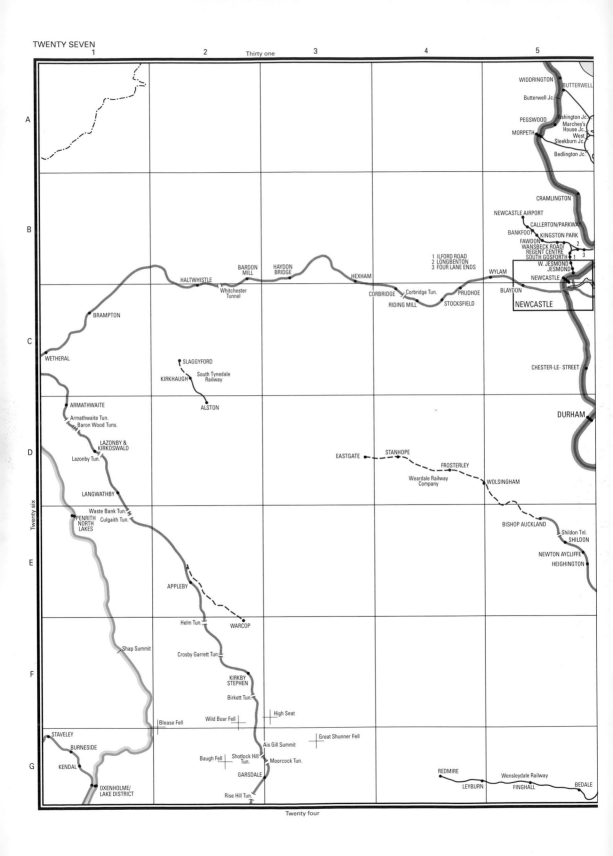

1   2   Thirty one   3   4   5

A

B

C

Twenty six

D

E

F

G

Twenty four

WIDDRINGTON
BUTTERWELL
Butterwell Jc.
Ashington Jc.
Marchey's House Jc.
PEGSWOOD
West Sleekburn Jc.
MORPETH
Bedlington Jc.

CRAMLINGTON
NEWCASTLE AIRPORT
CALLERTON/PARKWAY
BANKFOOT   KINGSTON PARK
FAWDON
WANSBECK ROAD/
REGENT CENTRE
SOUTH GOSFORTH
1 ILFORD ROAD
2 LONGBENTON
3 FOUR LANE ENDS
WYLAM
W. JESMOND
JESMOND
NEWCASTLE
BARDON MILL
HAYDON BRIDGE
HEXHAM
BLAYDON
HALTWHISTLE
NEWCASTLE
Whitchester Tunnel
CORBRIDGE   Corbridge Tun.   PRUDHOE
RIDING MILL   STOCKSFIELD
BRAMPTON

WETHERAL
CHESTER-LE- STREET

SLAGGYFORD
KIRKHAUGH   South Tynedale Railway

DURHAM
ARMATHWAITE
Armathwaite Tun.
Baron Wood Tuns.
ALSTON
LAZONBY & KIRKOSWALD
Lazonby Tun.
EASTGATE   STANHOPE
FROSTERLEY
Weardale Railway Company
WOLSINGHAM
LANGWATHBY

Waste Bank Tun.
PENRITH   Culgaith Tun.
NORTH LAKES
BISHOP AUCKLAND   Shildon Tnl.
SHILDON
NEWTON AYCLIFFE
HEIGHINGTON
APPLEBY

Helm Tun.   WARCOP
Shap Summit
Crosby Garrett Tun.

KIRKBY STEPHEN
Birkett Tun.
High Seat
Blease Fell   Wild Boar Fell
STAVELEY
BURNESIDE
Great Shunner Fell
Ais Gill Summit
KENDAL
Baugh Fell   Shotlock Hill Tun.   Moorcock Tun.
REDMIRE   Wensleydale Railway
GARSDALE
LEYBURN   FINGHALL   BEDALE
OXENHOLME/ LAKE DISTRICT
Rise Hill Tun.

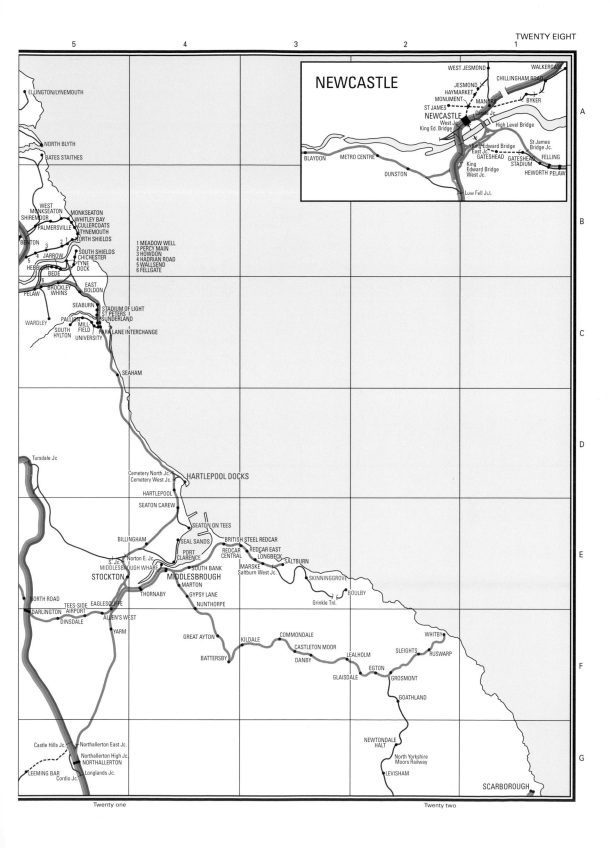

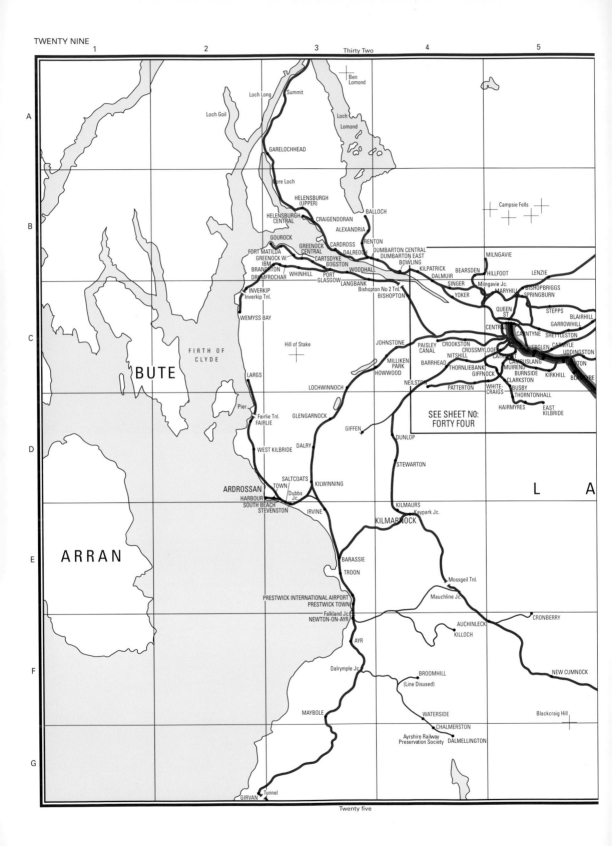

1   2   3   4   5

A

Ben Lomond

Loch Long   Summit

Loch Goil

Loch
Lomond

GARELOCHHEAD

Campsie Fells

B

Gare Loch

HELENSBURGH
(UPPER)

BALLOCH

HELENSBURGH   CRAIGENDORAN
CENTRAL

ALEXANDRIA

GOUROCK   RENTON

GREENOCK   CARDROSS   DUMBARTON CENTRAL   MILNGAVIE
FORT MATILDA   CENTRAL   DALREOCH   DUMBARTON EAST
GREENOCK W.   CARTSDYKE   BOWLING
IBM   BOGSTON   KILPATRICK   BEARSDEN   HILLFOOT   LENZIE
BRANCHTON   WODDHALL   DALMUIR
DRUMFROCHAR   WHINHILL   PORT   LANGBANK   SINGER   Mingavie Jc.
GLASGOW   Bishopton No 2 Tnl.   YOKER   MARYHILL   BISHOPBRIGGS
INVERKIP   BISHOPTON   SPRINGBURN
Inverkip Tnl.
QUEEN   STEPPS
WEMYSS BAY   ST   BLAIRHILL
CENTRAL   GARROWHILL

C   FIRTH OF   JOHNSTONE   CATHCART   CATKYLE
CLYDE   Hill of Stake   PAISLEY   CROOKSTON   CAMBUSLANG   CARMYLE
BUTE   CANAL   CROSSMYLOOF   RUTHERGLEN   SHETTLESTON
NITSHILL   CAMBUSLANG   UDDINGSTON
MILLIKEN   BARRHEAD   THORNLIEBANK   MUIREND   BURNSIDE   KIRKHILL
PARK   GIFFNOCK   CLARKSTON   BOTHWELL
LARGS   HOWWOOD   NEILSTON   BUSBY
LOCHWINNOCH   PATTERTON   WHITE-   THORNTONHALL
CRAIGS
Pier   HAIRMYRES   EAST
SEE SHEET NO: KILBRIDE
Fairlie Tnl.   GLENGARNOCK   FORTY FOUR
FAIRLIE   GIFFEN

D   WEST KILBRIDE   DALRY   DUNLOP

STEWARTON

L   A
SALTCOATS
TOWN   KILWINNING
ARDROSSAN   Dubbs
HARBOUR   Jc.   KILMAURS
SOUTH BEACH   IRVINE   Kaypark Jc.
STEVENSTON   KILMARNOCK

E   ARRAN   BARASSIE
TROON   Mossgeil Tnl.
PRESTWICK INTERNATIONAL AIRPORT   Mauchline Jc.
PRESTWICK TOWN   CRONBERRY
Falkland Jc.   AUCHINLECK
NEWTON-ON-AYR   KILLOCH
AYR

F   Dalrymple Jc.   BROOMHILL   NEW CUMNOCK
(Line Disused)

MAYBOLE   WATERSIDE   Blackcraig Hill

CHALMERSTON
Ayrshire Railway   DALMELLINGTON
Preservation Society

G   Tunnel
GIRVAN

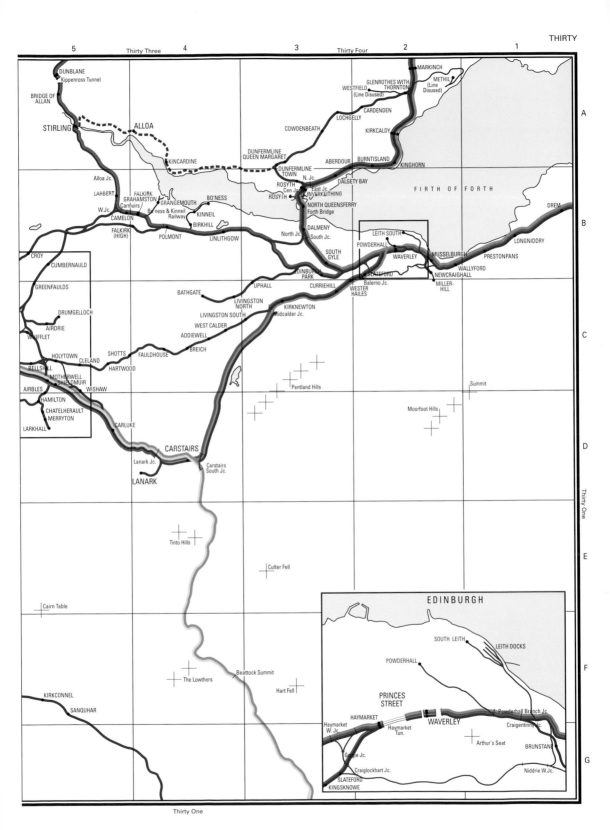

5   Thirty Three   4   3   Thirty Four   2   1

DUNBLANE
Kippenross Tunnel

BRIDGE OF
ALLAN

STIRLING   ALLOA

KINCARDINE

MARKINCH

GLENROTHES WITH
THORNTON
WESTFIELD   METHIL
(Line Disused)   (Line Disused)
CARDENDEN
LOCHGELLY
COWDENBEATH   KIRKCALDY

Alloa Jc.

LARBERT   FALKIRK
GRAHAMSTON
FALKIRK   GRANGEMOUTH   BO'NESS
W.Jc.   Carmuirs   Bo'ness & Kinneil
CAMELON   Railway   KINNEIL
FALKIRK   BIRKHILL
(HIGH)   POLMONT   LINLITHGOW

DUNFERMLINE
QUEEN MARGARET
DUNFERMLINE
TOWN
N. Jc.
ROSYTH   East Jc.
Cen Jc.   INVERKEITHING
ROSYTH   NORTH QUEENSFERRY
Forth Bridge

ABERDOUR   BURNTISLAND
KINGHORN

DALGETY BAY
DALMENY

FIRTH OF FORTH

DREM

North Jc.   South Jc.   LEITH SOUTH
POWDERHALL   WAVERLEY   MUSSELBURGH
SOUTH   EDINBURGH   SLATEFORD   NEWCRAIGHALL
GYLE   PARK   Balerno Jc.   MILLER-
CURRIEHILL   WESTER   HILL
UPHALL   HAILES

LONGNIDDRY
PRESTONPANS
WALLYFORD

CROY
CUMBERNAULD
GREENFAULDS

BATHGATE
LIVINGSTON
NORTH   KIRKNEWTON
LIVINGSTON SOUTH   Midcalder Jc.
WEST CALDER
ADDIEWELL
BREICH

DRUMGELLOCH
AIRDRIE
WHIFFLET
HOLYTOWN   SHOTTS   FAULDHOUSE
BELLSHILL   CLELAND
MOTHERWELL   HARTWOOD
SHIELDMUIR
AIRBLES   WISHAW
HAMILTON
CHATELHERAULT
MERRYTON
LARKHALL   CARLUKE

Pentland Hills

Summit

Moorfoot Hills

CARSTAIRS
Lanark Jc.   Carstairs
South Jc.
LANARK

Thirty One

Tinto Hills

Culter Fell

Cairn Table

KIRKCONNEL
SANQUHAR

Beattock Summit
The Lowthers   Hart Fell

EDINBURGH

SOUTH LEITH   LEITH DOCKS

POWDERHALL

PRINCES
STREET
HAYMARKET   Powderhall Branch Jc.
Haymarket   WAVERLEY
Haymarket   W. Jc.   Craigentinny Jc.
Tun.
Arthur's Seat   BRUNSTANE
Gorgie Jc.
Craiglockhart Jc.   Niddrie W. Jc.
SLATEFORD
KINGSKNOWE

1   2   3   4   5

A

Bass Rock

NORTH BERWICK

B   DUNBAR

St Abb's Head

Summit

C

BERWICK
Royal Border Bridge

D   Holy Island

Thirty

Eildon
Hills

E   CHATHILL

F   ALNMOUTH

ACKLINGTON

G   Peel Fell

WIDDRINGTON

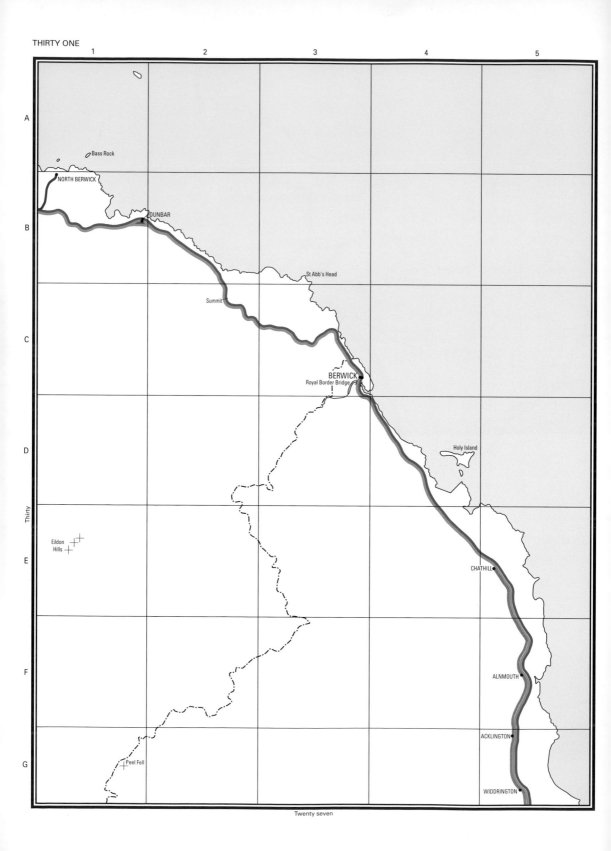

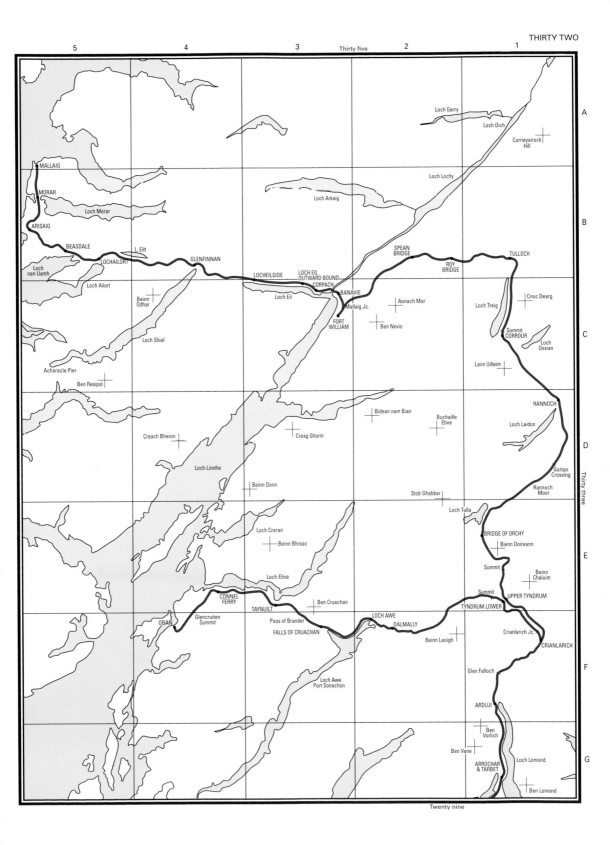

A

Loch Garry
Loch Oich
Corrieyairock
Hill

Loch Lochy

B

MALLAIG
Loch Arkaig
MORAR
Loch Morar
ARISAIG
BEASDALE
L. Eilt
SPEAN
BRIDGE
TULLOCH
Loch nan Uamh
LOCHAILORT
GLENFINNAN
ROY
BRIDGE
Loch Ailort
LOCHEILSIDE
LOCH EIL
OUTWARD BOUND
CORPACH
Cnoc Dearg
Beinn
Odhar
Loch Eil
BANAVIE
Aonach Mor
Loch Treig
Summit
CORROUR
Loch
Ossian
Mallaig Jc.
Loch Shiel
FORT
WILLIAM
Ben Nevis
Leim Uilleim

C

Acharacle Pier
Ben Resipol
RANNOCH
Bidean nam Bian
Buchaille
Etive
Loch Laidon
Creach Bheinn
Creag Ghorm

D

Loch Linnhe
Gortan
Crossing
Beinn Donn
Rannoch
Moor
Stob Ghabbar
Loch Tulla
Loch Creran
BRIDGE OF ORCHY
Beinn Bhreac
Bienn Doireann

E

Loch Etive
Summit
Beinn
Chaluim
Summit
UPPER TYNDRUM
CONNEL
FERRY
TAYNUILT
Ben Cruachan
TYNDRUM LOWER
Glencruiten
Summit
Pass of Brander
LOCH AWE
DALMALLY
Crianlarich Jc.
OBAN
FALLS OF CRUACHAN
Beinn Laoigh
CRIANLARICH

F

Loch Awe
Port Sonachan
Glen Falloch
ARDLUI
Ben
Vorlich

G

Ben Vane
Loch Lomond
ARROCHAR
& TARBET
Ben Lomond

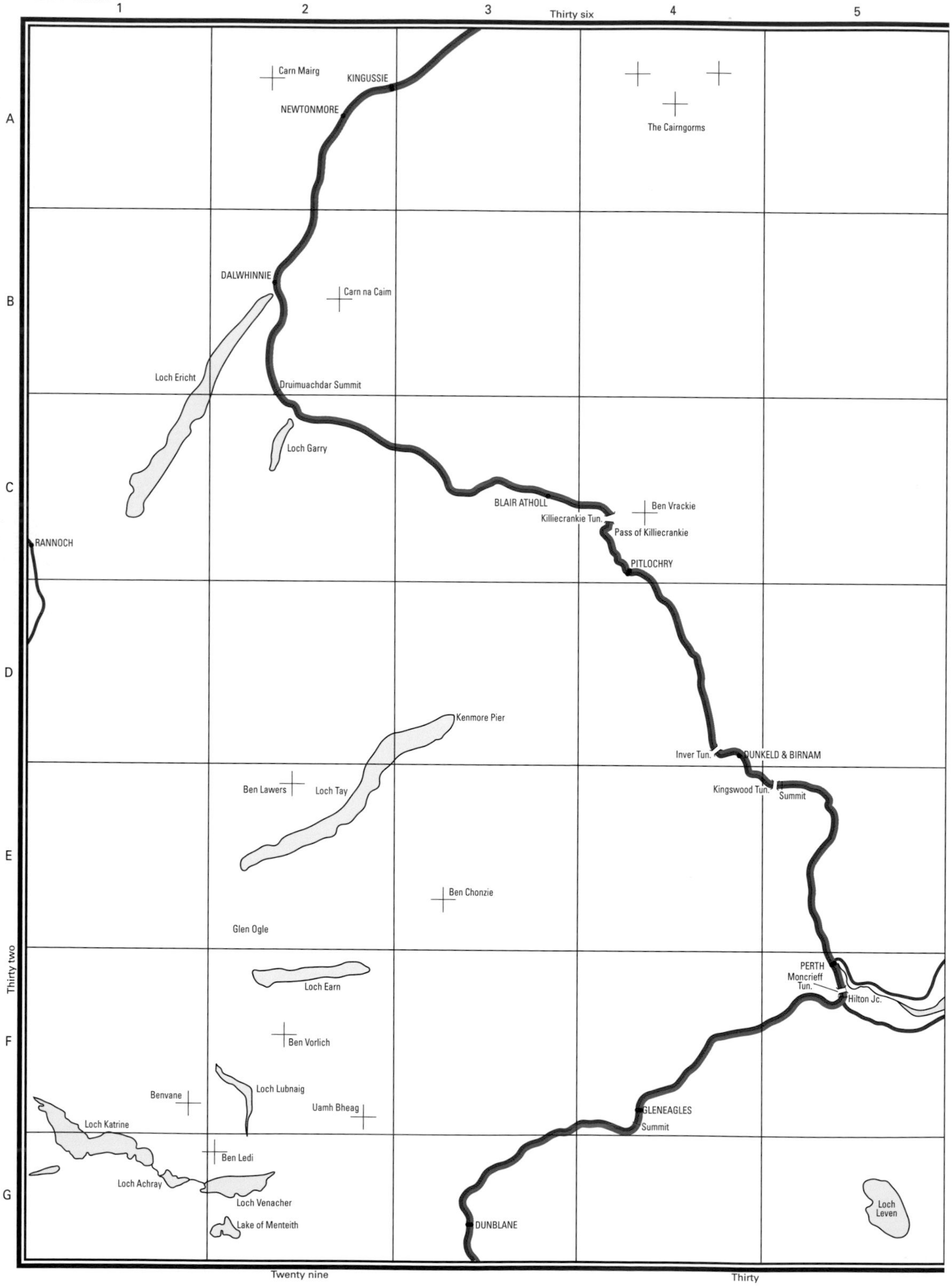

THIRTY THREE

1 2 3 Thirty six 4 5

A
+ Carn Mairg
KINGUSSIE
NEWTONMORE
+
+
The Cairngorms
+

B
DALWHINNIE
+ Carn na Caim
Loch Ericht
Druimuachdar Summit

C
Loch Garry
RANNOCH
BLAIR ATHOLL
Killiecrankie Tun. + Ben Vrackie
Pass of Killiecrankie
PITLOCHRY

D

Kenmore Pier
Inver Tun. DUNKELD & BIRNAM

E
Ben Lawers + Loch Tay
Kingswood Tun. Summit
+ Ben Chonzie
Glen Ogle

F
Loch Earn
PERTH
Moncrieff Tun.
Hilton Jc.
+ Ben Vorlich
Benvane + Loch Lubnaig
+ Uamh Bheag
Loch Katrine
GLENEAGLES
Summit
+ Ben Ledi
Loch Achray
Loch Venacher
Lake of Menteith
DUNBLANE
Loch Leven

G

Thirty two

Twenty nine Thirty

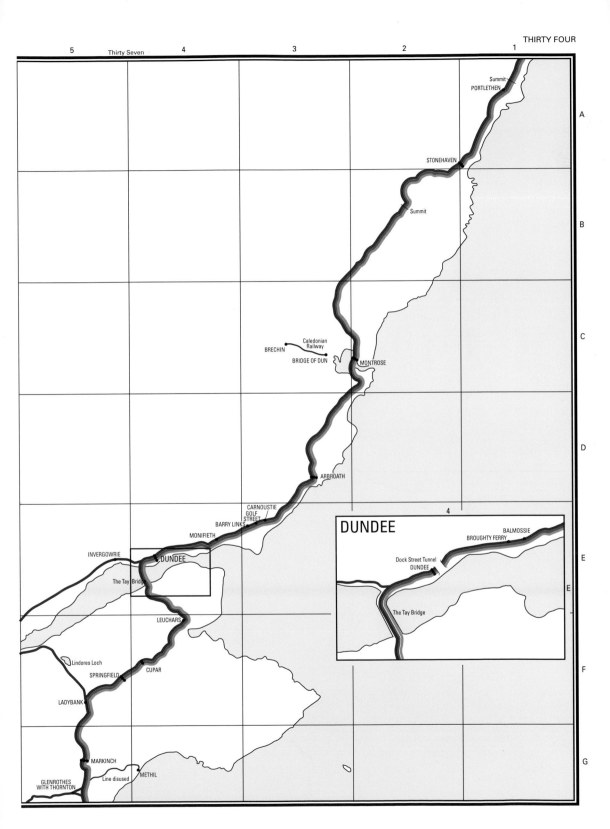

A

Summit
PORTLETHEN

STONEHAVEN

B

Summit

C

BRECHIN   Caledonian
Railway
BRIDGE OF DUN   MONTROSE

D

ARBROATH

CARNOUSTIE
GOLF
STREET
BARRY LINKS
MONIFIETH

INVERGOWRIE   DUNDEE
The Tay Bridge

E

DUNDEE

4

BALMOSSIE
BROUGHTY FERRY

Dock Street Tunnel
DUNDEE

The Tay Bridge

E

E

LEUCHARS

Lindores Loch
SPRINGFIELD   CUPAR

F

LADYBANK

MARKINCH
GLENROTHES
WITH THORNTON   Line disused   METHIL

G

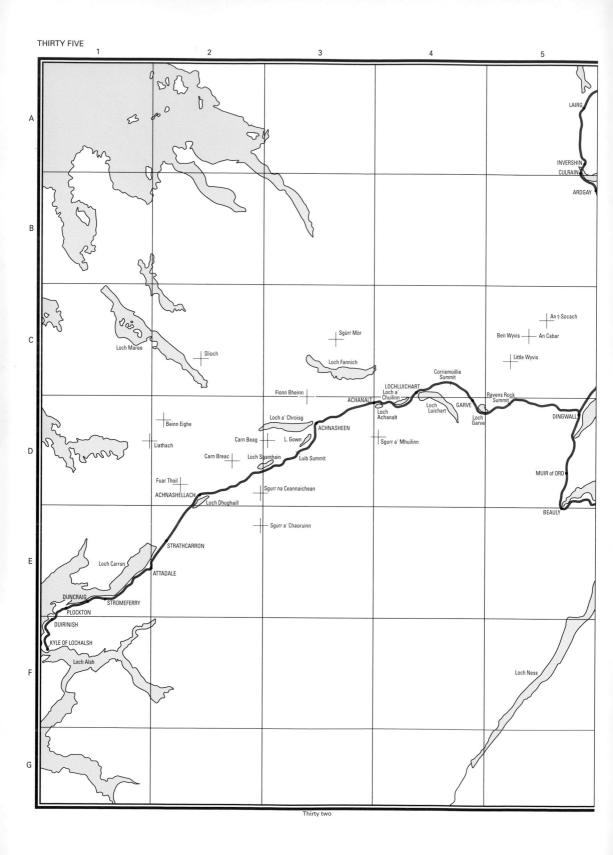

1   2   3   4   5

A

B

LAIRG

INVERSHIN
CULRAIN
ARDGAY

C

Loch Maree

Slioch

Sgùrr Mòr

Loch Fannich

An t-Socach

Ben Wyvis   An Cabar

Little Wyvis

Corriemoillie
Summit

Fionn Bheinn

LOCHLUICHART
Loch a'
Chuilinn

ACHANALT

Loch
Achanalt

Loch
Luichart

GARVE

Ravens Rock
Summit

DINGWALL

Loch a' Chroisg

ACHNASHEEN

Loch
Garve

Beinn Eighe

Carn Beag

L. Gown

Sgurr a' Mhuilinn

Liathach

D

Carn Breac

Loch Sgamhain

Luib Summit

Fuar Thoil

Sgurr na Ceannaichean

ACHNASHELLACH

Loch Dhughaill

MUIR of ORD

BEAULY

Sgurr a' Chaoruinn

STRATHCARRON

E

Loch Carron

ATTADALE

DUNCRAIG   STROMEFERRY
PLOCKTON
DUIRINISH
KYLE OF LOCHALSH

Loch Alsh

Loch Ness

F

G

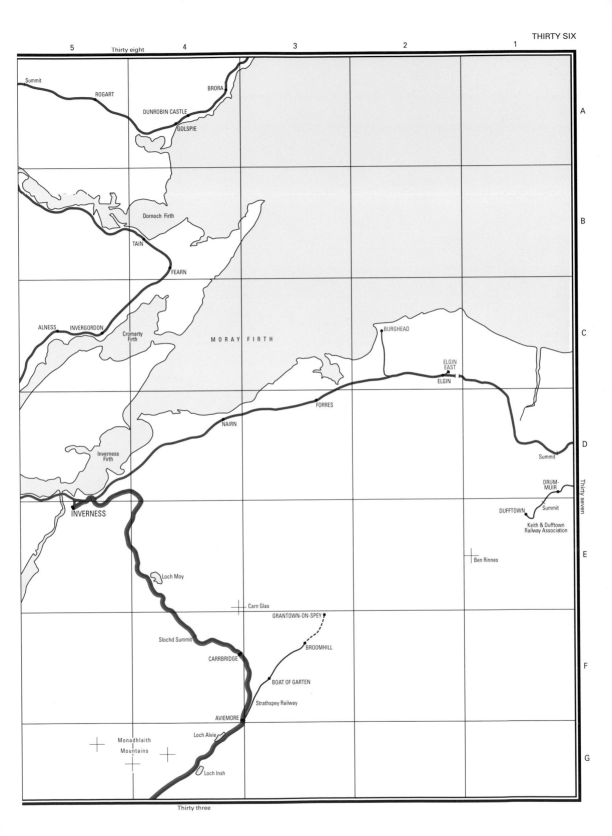

Summit
ROGART
BRORA
DUNROBIN CASTLE
GOLSPIE

A

Dornoch Firth

B

TAIN

FEARN

ALNESS   INVERGORDON
Cromarty
Firth

BURGHEAD

M O R A Y   F I R T H

ELGIN
EAST

ELGIN

C

FORRES

NAIRN

Inverness
Firth

Summit

D

DRUM-
MUIR

INVERNESS

DUFFTOWN   Summit

Keith & Dufftown
Railway Association

Ben Rinnes

E

Loch Moy

Carn Glas
GRANTOWN-ON-SPEY

Slochd Summit

BROOMHILL

CARRBRIDGE

F

BOAT OF GARTEN

Strathspey Railway

AVIEMORE

Loch Alvie

Monadhliath
Mountains

Loch Insh

G

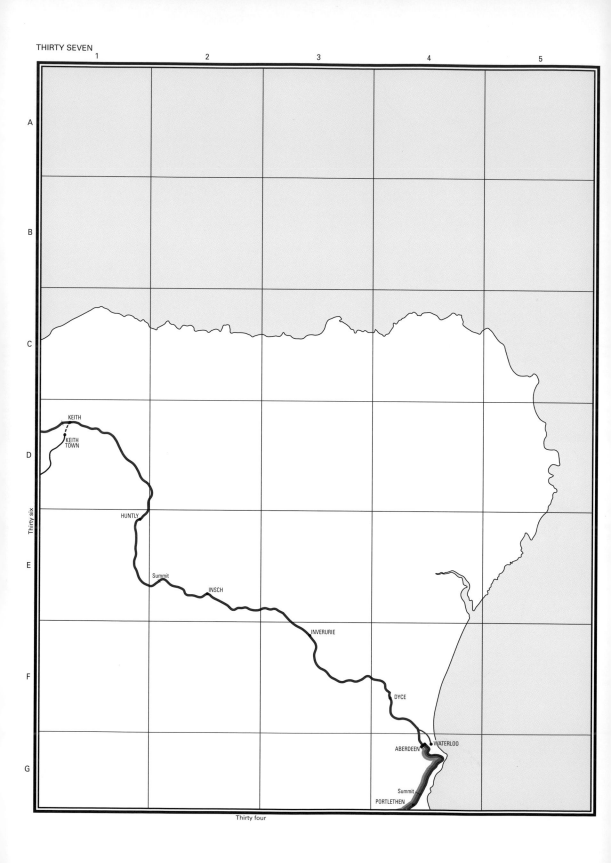

A

B

C

D

Thirty six

KEITH

KEITH
TOWN

HUNTLY

Summit

INSCH

INVERURIE

E

F

DYCE

ABERDEEN WATERLOO

G

Summit
PORTLETHEN

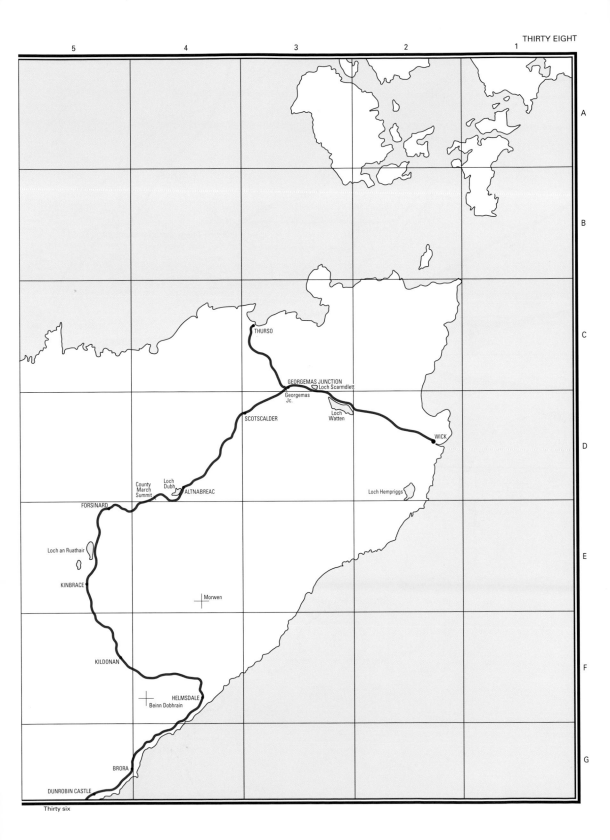

5   4   3   2   1

A

B

C

THURSO

GEORGEMAS JUNCTION
Loch Scarmdlett

Georgemas
Jc.

SCOTSCALDER

Loch
Watten

WICK

Loch Hempriggs

D

County
March
Summit

Loch
Dubh
ALTNABREAC

FORSINARD

Loch an Ruathair

E

KINBRACE

Morwen

KILDONAN

F

HELMSDALE
Beinn Dobhrain

BRORA

G

DUNROBIN CASTLE

1   2   3   4   5

PINNER

HARROW & WEALDSTONE

KENTON

QUEENSBURY

COLINDALE

HENDON CENTRAL

EAST FINCHLEY

A

NORTH HARROW

NORTHWICK PARK

KINGSBURY

HENDON

HIGHGATE WOOD SIDINGS

WEST HARROW

North Jc.   South Jc.

HARROW-ON-THE-HILL

SOUTH KENTON

PRESTON ROAD

BRENT CROSS

GOLDERS GREEN

NORTHERN LINE TO CENTRAL LONDON

EASTCOTE

RAYNERS LANE

SOUTH HARROW

NORTH WEMBLEY

SUDBURY HILL HARROW

WEMBLEY PARK

Dudding Jc.

CRICKLEWOOD

NORTHERN LINE TO CENTRAL LONDON

GOSPEL OAK

B

SOUTH RUISLIP

NORTHOLT PARK

SUDBURY HILL

SUDBURY & HARROW RD.

WEMBLEY STADIUM

Neasden S. Jc.

NEASDEN

DOLLIS HILL

WEST HAMPSTEAD THAMESLINK

WEST HAMPSTEAD & FROGNAL

FINCHLEY RD

HAMPSTEAD HEATH

Haverstock   Carlton Rd Jc.

NORTHOLT

WEMBLEY CENTRAL

SUDBURY TOWN

STONEBRIDGE PARK

Neasden Jc.

WILLESDEN GREEN

KILBURN

BRONDESBURY

Canfield Place (Hampstead Tun.)

SWISS COTTAGE

FINCHLEY RD

GREENFORD

ALPERTON

HARLESDEN

BRONDESBURY PARK

KENSAL RISE

QUEEN'S PARK

SOUTH HAMPSTEAD

KILBURN

St John's Wood Tun

Primrose Hill Tuns

ST. JOHN'S WOOD

SOUTH GREENFORD

PERIVALE

HANGER LANE

Brent Jc.

WILLESDEN JUNC.

Acton Wells Jc.

Old Oak Jc.

N. & S.W.

West London Jc.

KENSAL GREEN

Kensal Green Tuns

Kensal Green Jc.

Lords Tun.

GREAT PORTLAND ST

C

WESTBOURNE PARK

ROYAL OAK

CASTLE BAR PARK

PADDINGTON (H&C)

PADDINGTON

DRAYTON GREEN

PARK ROYAL

NORTH EALING

EALING BROADWAY

WEST ACTON

NORTH ACTON

Old Oak Common W. Jc.

Mitre Bri. Jc.

North Pole Jc.

NORTH POLE DEPOT

Portobello

Royal Oak

WESTBOURNE PARK

LADBROKE GROVE

LATIMER ROAD

MARYLEBONE

BAKER STREET

EDGWARE RD

PADDINGTON

Drayton Green Jc.

HANWELL

WEST EALING

EALING COMMON

ACTON MAINLINE

EAST ACTON

BAYSWATER

NOTTING HILL GATE

SOUTHALL

Hanwell Jc.

ACTON CENTRAL

SHEPHERDS BUSH

WHITE CITY

SHEPHERDS BUSH

HIGH ST KENSINGTON

VICTORIA

D

N. Jc.

ACTON TOWN

STH. ACTON

Acton Jc.

Bollo Lane Jc.

CHISWICK PARK

TURNHAM GREEN

STAMFORD BROOK

SHEPHERD'S BUSH

GOLDHAWK RD

CENTRAL LINE TO CENTRAL LONDON

KENSINGTON OLYMPIA

Cromwell Curve North Jc.

SLOANE SQUARE

SOUTH EALING

Brentford Lane Jc.

Acton Lane Jc.

RAVENSCOURT PARK

HAMMERSMITH

Cromwell Curve East Jc.

GLOUCESTER RD

STH. KENSINGTON

NORTHFIELDS

East Jc.

GUNNERSBURY

BARON'S COURT

WEST KENSINGTON

EARLS COURT

BOSTON MANOR

OSTERLEY

Old Jc.

KEW BRIDGE

New Jc.

CHISWICK

WEST BROMPTON

Battersea Wharf

BRENTFORD

BRENTFORD GOODS

KEW GARDENS

BARNES BRIDGE

FULHAM BROADWAY

PARSONS GREEN

BATTERSEA PARK

HOUNSLOW EAST

SYON LANE

BARNES

PUTNEY BRI.

IMPERIAL WHARF

QUEENSTOWN ROAD

HOUNSLOW WEST

HOUNSLOW CENTRAL

ISLEWORTH

RICHMOND

NORTH SHEEN

MORTLAKE

PUTNEY

WANDSWORTH TOWN

Latchmere Jcs

CLAPHAM JUNCTION

E

Hounslow Jc.

ST. MARGARETS

Battersea Pier Jc.

EAST PUTNEY

Point Pleasant Jc.

WANDSWORTH COMMON

Feltham Jc.

WHITTON

Whitton Jc.

TWICKENHAM

Latchmere S.W. Jc.

Latchmere Main Jc.

BATTERSEA PARK

Longhedge Jc.

QUEEN'S RD

SOUTHFIELDS

EARLSFIELD

BALHAM

Balham Jc.

STRAWBERRY HILL

CLAPHAM JUNCTION

Ludgate Jc.

Pouparts Jc.

Stewarts Lane Jc.

WIMBLEDON PARK

NORTHERN LINE TO CENTRAL LONDON

Strawberry Hill Jc.

Fulwell Jc.

FULWELL

Shacklegate Jc.

Falcon Jc.

Coal Yard Jc.

TOOTING BEC

KEMPTON PARK

STEWARTS LANE

Factory Jc.

WIMBLEDON

HAYDONS RD

TOOTING BROADWAY

TOOTING

F

HAMPTON

TEDDINGTON

KINGSTON

NORBITON

RAYNES PARK

DUNDONALD ROAD

WIMBLEDON CHASE

MERTON PARK

COLLIERS WOOD

SOUTH WIMBLEDON

MORDEN ROAD

HAMPTON WICK

NEW MALDEN

PHIPPS BRIDGE

BELGRAVE WALK

HAMPTON COURT

BERRYLANDS

MOTSPUR PARK

SOUTH MERTON

MORDEN

MITCHAM

THAMES DITTON

SURBITON

MALDEN MANOR

MORDEN SOUTH

MITCHAM JUNC.

G

Hampton Court Jc.

ST HELIER

ESHER

TOLWORTH

WORCESTER PARK

SUTTON COMMON

HACKBRIDGE

GREATER LONDON

DERBY & NOTTINGHAM TO SHEFFIELD

INFIRMARY ROAD
SHALESMOOR
CITY HALL
East Bank Tun.
ATTERCLIFFE
WOODBURN ROAD
DARNALL
NUNNERY SQUARE
Treeton Jc.
South Yorkshire Supertram
(Central Sheffield stations omitted)
SHEFFIELD
HOLLINSEND
GLEADLESS TOWNEND
HERDINGS LEIGHTON ROAD
HERDINGS PARK
BIRLEY MOOR ROAD
WHITE LANE
BIRLEY LANE
DONETSK WAY
MOSS WAY
HACKENTHORPE
CRYSTAL PEAKS
BEIGHTON
WATERTHORPE
WESTFIELD
HALFWAY
WOODHOUSE
Woodhouse Jc.
Beighton Jc.
Laughton E. Jc.
Dinnington Jc.
KIVETON BRIDGE
KIVETON PARK
Brancliffe Jc.
W. Jc.
E. Jc.
SHIREOAKS
S. Jc.
WORKSOP

DORE
Bradway Tun.
DRONFIELD
GRINDLEFORD
Broomhouse Tun.
CHESTERFIELD
OXCROFT
BOLSOVER

WHITWELL
Whitwell Tun.
CRESWELL
LANGWITH WHALEY THORNS
WELBECK COLLIERY
SHIREBROOK
EDWINSTOWE
Clipstone Jc.
CLIPSTONE COLLIERY
Clipstone Colliery Jc.
MANSFIELD WOODHOUSE
MANSFIELD
RUFFORD COLLIERY

ROWSLEY SOUTH
Peak Rail
DARLEY DALE
MATLOCK RIVERSIDE
MATLOCK
High Tor Tuns.
MATLOCK BATH
Willersley Tun.
CROMFORD
Clay Cross Tun.
SUTTON PARKWAY

WIRKSWORTH
Lea Wood Tun.
High Peak Jc.
WHATSTANDWELL
GORSEY BANK
Wyvern Rail
AMBERGATE
S. Jc.
Midland Railway Centre
BUTTERLEY
HAMMERSMITH
SWANWICK JUNCTION
ALFRETON
Alfreton Tun.
Wingfield Tun.
Codnor Park Jc.
BENTINCK
KIRKBY-IN-ASHFIELD
Kirkby Tun.
NEWSTEAD
HUCKNALL
CALVERTON
BUTLERS HILL
Bestwood Park Jc.
MOOR BRIDGE

BELPER
DENBY
LANGLEY MILL
BULWELL FOREST
BULWELL
Milford Tun.
DUFFIELD
(Line Disused)
PHOENIX PARK
CINDERHILL
HIGHBURY VALE
DAVID LANE
Nottingham Express Transit
BASFORD
NOEL STREET
GEDLING
BURTON JOYCE
CARLTON
Netherfield Jc.
NETHER- W. Jc.
FIELD
Little Eaton Jc.
Trowell Jc.
THE FOREST
Lenton Junctions
NOTTINGHAM
STANTON
BEESTON
ATTENBOROUGH
Toton Marshalling Yard
DERBY
SPONDON

1 WILKINSON STREET
2 RADFORD ROAD
3 HYSON GREEN MARKET
4 SHIPSTONE STREET
5 BEACONSFIELD STREET

NOTE: Other stops exist between
The Forest and Nottingham
Station

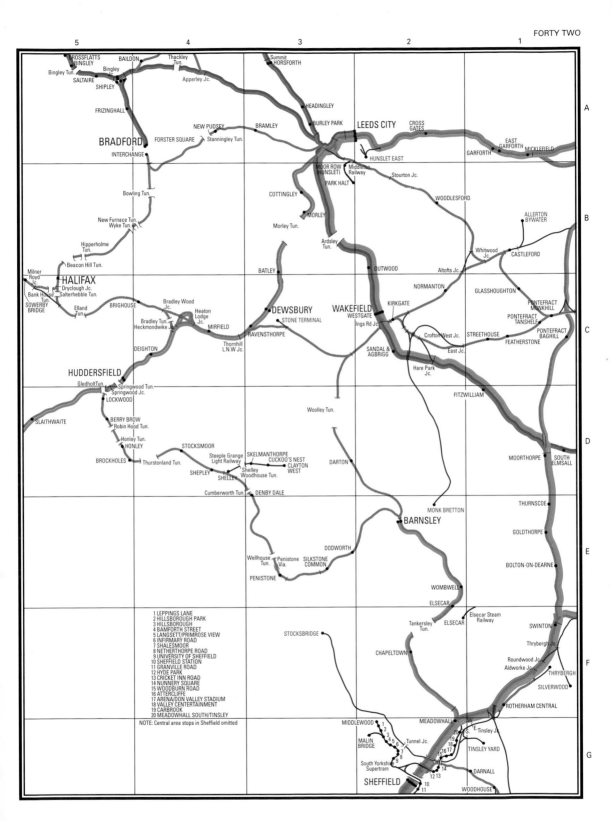

5   4   3   2   1

CROSSFLATTS
BINGLEY
BAILDON   Thackley
Bingley   Tun.
Bingley Tun.   Jc.
SALTAIRE   Apperley Jc.
SHIPLEY
FRIZINGHALL

Summit
HORSFORTH

A

NEW PUDSEY   BRAMLEY   BURLEY PARK   HEADINGLEY

BRADFORD   FORSTER SQUARE
INTERCHANGE   Stanningley Tun.

LEEDS CITY   CROSS
GATES   EAST
GARFORTH   MICKLEFIELD
GARFORTH
HUNSLET EAST

MOOR ROW
(HUNSLET)   Middleton
Railway
PARK HALT   Stourton Jc.
Bowling Tun.   WOODLESFORD

COTTINGLEY   ALLERTON
BYWATER   B
New Furnace Tun.   MORLEY
Wyke Tun.   Morley Tun.   Whitwood   CASTLEFORD
Jc.
Hipperholme
Tun.   Ardsley
Tun.
Beacon Hill Tun.   BATLEY   OUTWOOD   Altofts Jc.
Milner   HALIFAX
Royd   Dryclough Jc.   NORMANTON   GLASSHOUGHTON
Jc.   Salterhebble Tun.
Bank House   PONTEFRACT
Tun.   Elland   BRIGHOUSE   Bradley Wood   DEWSBURY   WAKEFIELD   KIRKGATE   MONKHILL
SOWERBY   Jc.   Jc.   WESTGATE   PONTEFRACT
BRIDGE   STONE TERMINAL   TANSHELF
Bradley Tun.   Heaton   Ings Rd Jc.   PONTEFRACT   C
Heckmondwike Jc.   Lodge   Crofton West Jc.   STREETHOUSE   BAGHILL
Jc.   MIRFIELD   RAVENSTHORPE   FEATHERSTONE
DEIGHTON   Thornhill   SANDAL &   East Jc.
L.N.W Jc.   AGBRIGG
HUDDERSFIELD   Hare Park
Jc.
Gledholt Tun.   Springwood Tun.   Woolley Tun.   FITZWILLIAM
Springwood Jc.
SLAITHWAITE   LOCKWOOD
BERRY BROW
Robin Hood Tun.   MOORTHORPE   SOUTH
ELMSALL   D
Honley Tun.   STOCKSMOOR
BROCKHOLES   HONLEY   Steeple Grange   SKELMANTHORPE
Thurstonland Tun.   Light Railway   CUCKOO'S NEST
SHEPLEY   Shelley   CLAYTON
SHELLEY   Woodhouse Tun.   WEST   DARTON
Cumberworth Tun.   DENBY DALE
THURNSCOE
MONK BRETTON
GOLDTHORPE
BARNSLEY
DODWORTH   BOLTON-ON-DEARNE   E
Wellhouse   Penistone   SILKSTONE
Tun.   Via.   COMMON
PENISTONE   WOMBWELL
ELSECAR
Elsecar Steam
Tankersley   ELSECAR   Railway   SWINTON
Tun.
STOCKSBRIDGE   Thrybergh Jc.   F
CHAPELTOWN
Roundwood Jc.
Aldworke Jc.   THRYBERGH
SILVERWOOD
ROTHERHAM CENTRAL

1 LEPPINGS LANE
2 HILLSBOROUGH PARK
3 HILLSBOROUGH
4 BAMFORTH STREET
5 LANGSETT/PRIMROSE VIEW
6 INFIRMARY ROAD
7 SHALESMOOR
8 NETHERTHORPE ROAD
9 UNIVERSITY OF SHEFFIELD
10 SHEFFIELD STATION
11 GRANVILLE ROAD
12 HYDE PARK
13 CRICKET INN ROAD
14 NUNNERY SQUARE
15 WOODBURN ROAD
16 ATTERCLIFFE
17 ARENA/DON VALLEY STADIUM
18 VALLEY CENTERTAINMENT
19 CARBROOK
20 MEADOWHALL SOUTH/TINSLEY

NOTE: Central area stops in Sheffield omitted

MIDDLEWOOD   MEADOWHALL   W
1   S.
2   E. Tinsley Jc.
3   Tunnel Jc.
MALIN   4 5
BRIDGE   5 6   20   TINSLEY YARD
7   16 17   18
South Yorkshire   8   15   14
Supertram   9   12 13   DARNALL   G
10
11   WOODHOUSE
SHEFFIELD

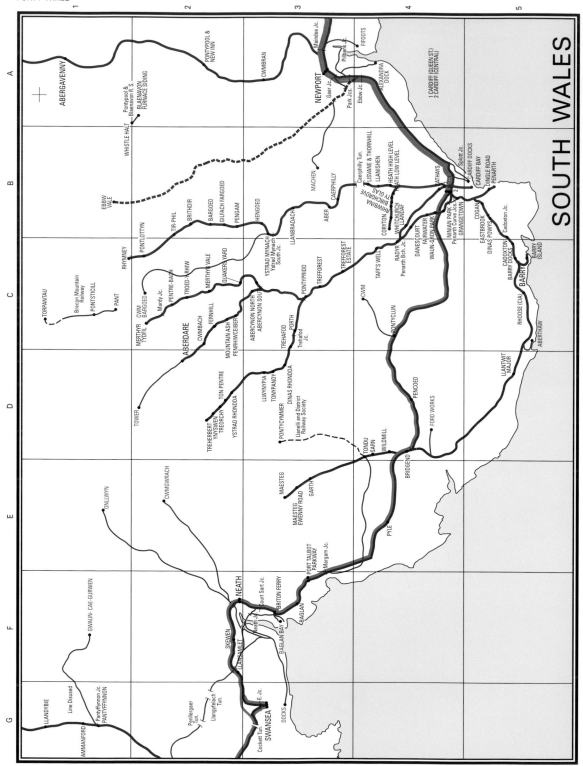

1
2
3
4
5

SOUTH WALES

ABERGAVENNY

WHISTLE HALT
Pontypool & Blaenavon R. S.
BLAENAVON FURNACE SIDING
PONTYPOOL & NEW INN
CWMBRAN

NEWPORT
Maindee Jc.
Pilbank Jc.
FFOOTS

Gaer Jc.
Park Jcs.
Ebbw Jc.
ALEXANDRA DOCK

1 CARDIFF (QUEEN ST)
2 CARDIFF (CENTRAL)

EBBW VALE

Caerphilly Tun.
LISVANE & THORNHILL
LLANISHEN
HEATH HIGH LEVEL
HEATH LOW LEVEL

MACHEN
CAERPHILLY

ABER

RHYMNEY
PONTLOTTYN
TIR-PHIL
BRITHDIR
BARGOED
GILFACH FARGOED
PENGAM
HENGOED

LLANBRADACH

TREFFOREST ESTATE

RHIWBINA
BIRCHGROVE
TY GLAS

CORYTON
WHITCHURCH
LLANDAF

CATHAYS
SPLOTT Jc.
CARDIFF DOCKS
DINGLE ROAD
PENARTH
CARDIFF BAY

PENTRE-BACH
Mardy Jc.
MERTHYR VALE
TROED-Y-RHIW
QUAKERS YARD

YSTRAD MYNACH
Ystrad Mynach South Jc.

PONTYPRIDD
TREFFOREST

TAFF'S WELL

RADYR
Penarth Bch. Jc.

DANESCOURT
FAIRWATER
WAUN-GRON PARK

NINIAN PARK
Penarth Curve Jcs.
GRANGETOWN
COGAN
EASTBROOK
DINAS POWYS
Cadoxton Jc.

PANT
TORPANTAU
Brecon Mountain Railway
PONTSTICILL

MERTHYR TYDFIL
CWM BARGOED
CWMBACH
FERNHILL

MOUNTAIN ASH
PENRHIWCEIBER

ABERCYNON NORTH
ABERCYNON SOU

TREHAFOD
PORTH
Trehafod Jc.

CWM

PONTYCLUN

CADOXTON
RHOOSE (CIA)
BARRY DOCKS
BARRY
BARRY ISLAND

ABERDARE

TOWER

TREHERBERT
YNYSWEN
TREORCHY
TON PENTRE
YSTRAD RHONDDA

LLWYNYPIA
TONYPANDY
DINAS RHONDDA

PONTYCYMMER

Llanelli and District Railway Society

PENCOED

FORD WORKS

ABERTHAW

LLANTWIT MAJOR

CWMGWRACH

ONLLWYN

MAESTEG
MAESTEG EWENNY ROAD
GARTH

TONDU
SARN
WILDMILL

BRIDGEND

PYLE

LLANDYBIE
Line Disused
AMMANFORD
GWAUN-CAE-GURWEN
Pantyffynnon Jc.
PANTYFFYNNON

Penllergaer Tun.
Llangyfelach Tun.
E. Jc.
SKEWEN
LLANSAMLET
Neath Jc.
Court Sart Jc.
BRITON FERRY
BAGLAN BAY
BAGLAN

NEATH

PORT TALBOT PARKWAY
Margam Jc.

Cockett Tun.
SWANSEA
DOCKS

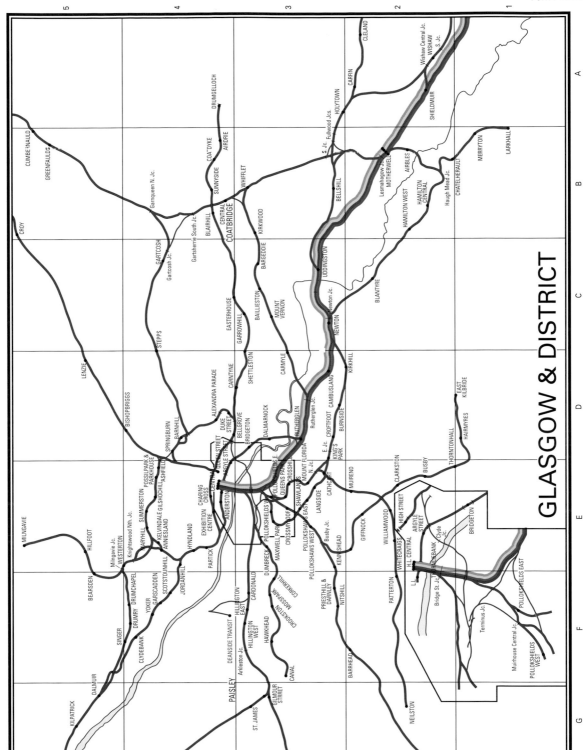

GLASGOW & DISTRICT

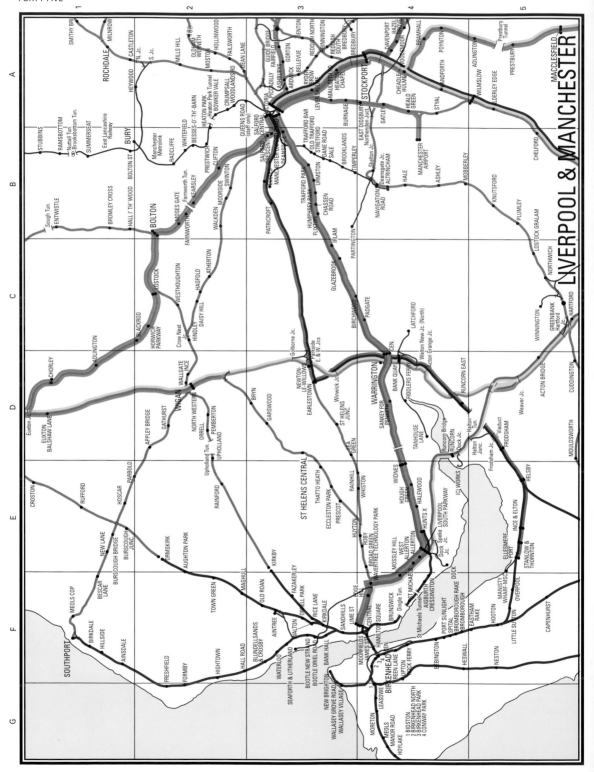

LIVERPOOL & MANCHESTER

INDEX TO PASSENGER STATIONS

Note: Ownership/control of stations is indicated in brackets as follows:

AW	Arriva Trains Wales	IoM	Isle of Man	SN	Southern
CC	c2c	LE	'one'	SE	South Eastern Trains
CH	Chiltern	LT	London for Transport	SL	Silverlink
CT	Central Trains	ME	Merseyrail	SR	First ScotRail
CTL	Croydon Tramlink	Metrolink	Manchester Metrolink	SW	South West Trains
DLR	Docklands Light Railway	Midland Metro	Midland Metro	SYS	South Yorkshire Supertram
FC	First Capital Connect	ML	Midland Main Line	TP	Transpennine Express
GR	Great North Eastern	NET	Nottingham Express Transit	T&W	Tyne & Wear Metro (Nexus)
GW	First Greater Western	NT	Northern	VT	Virgin Trains
HX	Heathrow Express	NW	Network Rail	WA	West Anglia Great Northern
IL	Island Line	Pres	Preservation Society		

Abbey Wood (SE) 5B4
Aber (AW) 8B4/43B3
Abercynon North (AW) 8B5/43C3
Abercynon South (AW) 8B5/43C3
Aberdare (AW) 8B5/43D2
Aberdeen (SR) 37G4
Aberdour (SR) 30B3
Aberdovey (AW) 13B5
Aberech (AW) 19F1
Abergavenny (AW) 8A3/43A1
Abergele & Pensarn (AW) 19D5
Abergynolwyn (Pres) 13B5
Aberystwyth (AW) 13C5
Accrington (NT) 24D1
Achanalt (SR) 35D3
Achnasheen (SR) 35D3
Achnashellach (SR) 35D2
Acklington (NT) 31G5
Acle (LE) 18E2
Acocks Green (CT) 9A5/15G5
Acton Bridge (CT) 15A1/20D2/45B5
Acton Central (SL) 39C3
Acton Main Line (GW) 39C3
Acton Town (LT) 39D3
Adderley Park (CT) 13C4
Addiewell (SR) 30C4
Addington Village (CTL) 5C4
Addiscombe (CTL) 40G4
Addlestone (SW) 5C2
Adisham (SE) 6C2
Adlington (NT) 15A3/20C1/45A5
Adwick (NT) 21F5
Aigburth (ME) 45F4
Ainsdale (ME) 20A4/24E4/45F1
Aintree (ME) 20B4/24F4/45F3
Airbles (SR) 44B2
Airdrie (SR) 30C5/44A4
Albany Park (SE) 5B4
Albrighton (CT) 15F3
Alderley Edge (NT) 15A3/20D1/45A5
Aldermaston (GW) 4A3
Aldershot (SW) 4B1
Aldgate (LT) 40D4
Aldgate East (LT) 40D4
Aldrington (SN) 5F3
Alexandra Palace (FC) 44D4
Alexandra Parade (SR) 44D4
Alexandria (SR) 29B3
Alfreton (CT) 16C4/41E3
All Saints (DLR) 40C3
Allen's West (NT) 28F5

Alloa (SR; proposed) 30A4
Alness (SR) .36C5
Alnmouth (NT) 31F5
Alperton (LT) 39B2
Alresford (Essex) (LE) 12E4
Alresford (Hants) (Pres) 4C3
Alsager (CT) 15C3/20E1
Althorne (LE) 12G5
Althorpe (NT) 22F5
Altnabreac (SR) 38D4
Alton (SW) .4C2
Altrincham (NT) 15A3/20C1/24G1/45B4
Alvechurch (CT) 9A4
Ambergate (CT) 16C5/41E2
Amberley (SN) 5F1
Amersham (LT) 10F1
Amlwch (Pres; proposed) 19C1
Ammanford (AW) 7A3/43G1
Ampere Way (CTL) 40G5
Ancaster (CT) 16C1/17C1
Anderston (SR) 44E4
Andover (SW) 4C4
Anerley (SN) 40F4
Angel Road (WN) 5A3
Angmering (SN) 5F2
Annan (SR) .26B2
Anniesland (SR) 44E4
Ansdell & Fairhaven (NT) 20A4/24E4
Appleby (NT) 27E2
Appledore (SN) 6E4
Appleford (GW) 10F4
Appley Bridge (NT) 20B3/24F3/45D2
Apsley (SL) .11F1
Arbroath (SR) 34D3
Ardgay (SR) 36B5
Ardlui (SR) .32F1
Ardrossan Harbour (SR) 29D3
Ardrossan South Beach (SR) 29D3
Ardrossan Town (SR) 29D3
Ardwick (NT) 20B1/45A3
Arena (CTL) 40G4
Arena/Don Valley Stadium (SYS) 42G2
Argyle Street (SR) 44E2
Arisaig (SR) .32B5
Arlesey (FC) 11D2
Arley (Pres) .9A2
Armathwaite (NT) 27D1
Arnside (TP) 24A3
Arram (NT) .22D4
Arrochar & Tarbet (SR) 32G1
Arundel (SN) 5F1

Ascot (SW) 4A1/5B1
Ascott under Wychwood (GW) 10D5
Ash (SW) 4B1/5C1
Ash Vale (SW) 4B1/5C1
Ashburys (NT) 20B1/20F1/45A3
Ashchurch (GW) 9D3
Ashey (Pres) .4F3
Ashfield (SR) 44E4
Ashford (Surrey) (SW) 5B2
Ashford International (SE) 6D4
Ashley (NT) 15A3/20C1/24G1/45B4
Ashtead (SN) 5C2
Ashton under Lyne (NT) 21F1
Ashurst (SN) 5D4
Ashurst New Forest (SW) 4E4
Ashwell & Morden (FC) 11D2
Askam (NT) .24A5
Aslockton (CT) 16C2
Aspatria (NT) 26D3
Aspley Guise (SL) 10C1
Aston (CT) 13B4/15G4
Atherstone (CT) 16F5
Atherton (NT) 20B2/24F2/45C2
Attadale (SR) 35D2
Attenborough (CT) 16D4/41G4
Attercliffe (SYS) 41A2/42G2
Attleborough (LE) 12A4/18F4
Auchinleck (SR) 29F5
Audley End (LE) 11E4
Aughton Park (ME) 20B4/24F3/45E2
Avenue Road (CTL) 40F4
Aviemore (SR) 36F4
Avoncliff (GW) 3B4
Avonmouth (GW) 3A2/8C2/9G1
Axminster (SW) 2B1
Aylesbury (CH) 10E2
Aylesford (SE) 6C5
Aylesham (SE) 6C2
Aylsham (Pres) 18D3
Ayr (SR) 29F3

Bache (ME) .20D4
Baglan (AW) 43F3
Bagshot (SW) 5C1
Baildon (NT) 21D2/42A4
Baillieston (SR) 29C5/44C3
Baker Street (LT) 39C5
Bala (Pres) 19F4
Balcombe (SN) 5E3
Baldock (FC) 11E2
Balham (SN) 5B3/39E5

Ballabeg (IoM) .23C2
Ballasalla (IoM) 23C2
Balloch (SR) 29B3
Balmossie (SR) .34E4
Bamber Bridge (NT) 20A3/24E3
Bamford (NT) 15A5
Bamforth Street (SYS) 42G2
Banavie (SR) 32C3
Banbury (CH) 10C4
Bangor (AW) 19D2
Bank Hall (ME) .45F3
Bankfoot (T&W) 27B5
Banstead (SN) 5C3
Barassie (SR) 29E3
Barbican (LT) 40D5
Bardon Mill (NT) 27B2
Bare Lane (NT) .24B3
Bargeddie (SR) 29C5/44C3
Bargoed (AW) 8B4/43B2
Barking (CC) 5A4/40B1
Barkingside (LT) 40A1
Barlaston (CT) 15D3/20F1
Barming (SE) 6C5
Barmouth (AW) .13A5
Barnehurst (SE) 5B4
Barnes (SW) 5B339E4
Barnes Bridge (SW) 39D3
Barnetby (TP) 22F3
Barnham (SN) 5F1
Barnhill (SR) 44D4
Barnsley (NT) 21F3/42E2
Barnstaple (GW) .7F3
Barnt Green (CT) 9A4
Barons Court (LT) 39D4
Barrhead (SR) 29C4/44F3
Barrhill (SR) 25A3
Barrow Haven (NT) 22E3
Barrow in Furness (TP) 24B5
Barrow upon Soar (CT) 16E4
Barry (AW) 8D4/43B5
Barry Docks (AW) 8D4/43B5
Barry Island (AW) 8D4/43B5
Barry Links (SR) 34E4
Barton on Humber (NT) 22E4
Basford (NET) 41F4
Basildon (CC) 6A5
Basingstoke (SW) 4B2
Bat & Ball (SE) .5C4
Bath Spa (GW) 3A3/8D1
Bathgate (SR) 30C4
Batley (NT) 21E342B3
Battersby (NT) 28F4
Battersea Park (SN) 39D5
Battle (SE) 6F5
Battlesbridge (LE) 6A5/11G5
Bayford (FC) 11F2
Bayswater (LT) .39C5
Beaconsfield (CH) 5A110F1
Beaconsfield Street (NET) 41F4
Bearley (CT) 9B5
Bearsden (SR) 29B4/44F5
Bearsted (SE) 6C5
Beasdale (SR) 32B5
Beaulieu Road (SW) 4E4
Beauly (SR) 35E5
Bebington (ME) 20C4/24G4/45F4
Beccles (LE) 12A2/18G2
Beckenham Hill (SE) 40F3
Beckenham Junction (SE; CTL) 40F3
Beckenham Road (CTL) 40F4

Beckfoot (Pres) .26F2
Beckton (DLR) .40C1
Beckton Park (DLR) 40C1
Bedale (Pres) 27G5
Beddgelert (Pres) 19E2
Beddington Lane (CTL) 40G5
Bede (T&W) 28B5
Bedford (FC) 10C1
Bedford St Johns (SL) 10C1/11D1
Bedhampton (SW) 4E2
Bedminster (GW) 3A2
Bedworth (CT) .16G5
Bedwyn (GW) 4A5
Beeston (CT) 16D4/41G4
Beighton (SYS) .41A3
Bekesbourne (SE) 6C2
Belgrave Walk (CTL) 39G5
Belle Vue (NT) 20C1/24G1/45A3
Bellgrove (SR) 44D4
Bellingham (SE) .40F3
Bellshill (SR) 30C5/44B3
Belmont (SN) 5C3
Belper (CT) 16C5/41F2
Beltring (SE) 5C5
Belvedere (SE) 5B4
Bempton (NT) 22B3
Ben Rhydding (NT) 21C2
Benfleet (CC) 6A5
Bentham (NT) 24B2
Bentley (S. Yorks) (NT) 21F5
Bentley (SW) 4C1
Benton (T&W) .27B5
Bere Alston (GW) 1D5
Bere Ferrers (GW) 1D5
Berkhamsted (SL) 10E1
Berkswell (CT) 9A5
Berney Arms (LE) 18F1
Berry Brow (NT) 21E2/42D5
Berrylands (SW) 39G3
Berwick (SN) 5F4
Berwick-upon-Tweed (GR) 31C3
Berwyn (Pres) 20F5
Bescar Lane (NT) 20A4/24E4/45F1
Bescot Stadium (CT) 13A3/15F4
Besses-o'-th'-Barn (Metrolink) 45B2
Betchworth (SW) 5C2
Bethnal Green (LE) 40C4
Betws-y-Coed (AW) 19E4
Beverley (NT) 22D4
Bewdley (Pres) 9A2
Bexhill (SN) 6F5
Bexley (SE) 5B4
Bexleyheath (SE) 5B4
Bickley (SE) 40G2
Bicester North (CH) 10D3
Bicester Town (GW) 10D3
Bidston (ME) 20C4/24G4/45G4
Biggleswade (FC) 11D2
Bilbrook (CT) 15F3
Billericay (LE) 5A511G5
Billingham (NT) 28E4
Billingshurst (SN) 5E2
Bilston Central (Midland Metro) 13A2
Bingham (CT) 16C3
Bingley (NT) 21D2/42A5
Birchgrove (AW) 43B4
Birchington on Sea (SE) 6B2
Birchwood (TP) 20C2
Birkbeck (SN; CTL) 40F4
Birkdale (ME) 20A4/24E4/45F1

Birkenhead (ME) 20C4/24G4/45F4
Birkenhead Central (ME) 45F4
Birkenhead North (ME) 45F4
Birkenhead Park (ME) 45F4
Birkhill (Pres) 30B4
Birley Lane (SYS) 41A2
Birley Moor Road (SYS) 41A2
Birmingham International (VT) 9A5
Birmingham Moor Street (CH) . . .13C4/15G4
Birmingham New Street (NW) . . .13C3/15G4
Birmingham Snow Hill (CT) 13C3/15G4
Bishop Auckland (NT) 27E5
Bishop's Lydeard (Pres) 8F4
Bishopbriggs (SR) 29C5/44D4
Bishops Stortford (LE) 11E3
Bishopstone (SN) 5G4
Bishopton (SR) .29C4
Bitterne (SW) 4E4
Bitton (Pres) 8D1
Black Lane (Midland Metro) 13B2
Blackburn (NT) .24D2
Blackheath (SE) 5B4/40E2
Blackhorse Lane (CTL) 40G4
Blackhorse Road (SL) 40A3
Blackpool North (NT) 24D4
Blackpool Pleasure Beach (NT) 24D4
Blackpool South (NT) 24D4
Blackrod (NT) 20B2/24F2/45D1
Blackwall (DLR) 40C3
Blackwater (GW) 4B1
Blaenau Ffestiniog (AW) 19F3
Blaenavon (Pres) 8A4
Blair Atholl (SR) 33C3
Blairhill (SR) 29C5/44B4
Blake Street (CT) 15F5
Blakedown (CT) .9A3
Blantyre (SR) 29C5/44C2
Blaydon (NT) 27C5/28A3
Bleasby (CT) 16C3
Bletchley (SL) 10D2
Blodwell (Pres; proposed) 20G5
Bloxwich (CT) 15F4
Bloxwich North (CT) 15F4
Blue Anchor (Pres) 8E5
Blundellsands & Crosby (ME)20B4/24F4/45F3
Blunsdon (Pres) .9F5
Blythe Bridge (CT) 15C4
Bo'ness (Pres) 30B4
Boat of Garten (Pres) 36F3
Bodmin General (Pres) 1D3/6F5
Bodmin Parkway (GW) 1D3
Bodorgan (AW) .19D1
Bognor Regis (SN) 5G1
Bogston (SR) 29B3
Bolton (NT) 20B2/24F2/45B2
Bolton Abbey (Pres) 21C1
Bolton on Dearne (NT) 21F4/42E1
Bookham (SW) .5C2
Bootle (NT) 24A5/26G3
Bootle New Strand (ME) 45A3
Bootle Oriel Road (ME) 45A3
Bordesley (CT) 13C4/15G4
Borough Green & Wrotham (SE) 5C5
Borth (AW) 13C5
Boscarne Junction (Pres) 1D3
Bosham (SN) 4E1
Boston (CT) 17C3
Boston Manor (LT) 39D2
Botley (SW) 4E3
Bottesford (CT) .16D2

Bourne End (GW) 5A1/10G2
Bournemouth (SW) 3F5
Bournville (CT) 9A4
Bow Brickhill (SL) 10D2
Bowes Park (WN) 5A3
Bowling (SR) 29B4
Bow Church (LT) 40C3
Bow Road (DLR) 40C3
Boxhill & Westhumble (SN) 5C2
Bracknell (SW) 4A1
Bradford Forster Square (NT) 21D2/42A4
Bradford Interchange (NT) 21D2/42A4
Bradford on Avon (GW) 3B4
Brading (IL) 4F3
Bradley Lane (Midland Metro) 13A2
Braintree (LE) 11E5
Braintree Freeport (LE) 11E5
Bramhall (NT) 15A3/20C1/45A4
Bramley (NT) 21D2/42A3
Bramley (Hants) (GW) 4B2
Brampton (Cumbria) (NT) 27C1
Brampton (Pres) 18E3
Brampton (Suffolk) (LE) 12B2
Branchton (SR) 29B2
Brandon (LE) 11A5/17G5
Branksome (SW) 3F5
Braystones (NT) 26F3
Brechin (Pres) 34C3
Bredbury (NT) 21G1
Breich (SR) 30C4
Brent Cross (LT) 5A3
Brentford (SW) 5B2/39D2
Brentwood (LE) 5A5
Bricket Wood (SL) 11G1
Bridge of Allan (SR) 30A5
Bridge of Dun (Pres) 34C3
Bridge of Orchy (SR) 32E1
Bridgend (AW) 7C5/43D4
Bridgeton (SR) 44D3
Bridgnorth (Pres) 15F2
Bridgwater (GW) 3C1/8F3
Bridlington (NT) 22B3
Brierfield (NT) 24D1
Brigg (NT) 22F4
Brighouse (NT) 21E2, 42C4
Brighton (SN) 5F3
Brimsdown (LE) 11G3
Brinnington (NT) 45A3
Bristol Parkway (GW) 8C1/9G1
Bristol Temple Meads (GW) 3A2/8C2
Brithdir (AW) 8B4/43B2
British Steel (Redcar) (NT) 28E4
Briton Ferry (AW) 7B4/43F3
Brixton (SE) 5B3/40E5
Broad Green (NT) 45E4
Broadbottom (NT) 21G1
Broadstairs (SE) 6B1
Brockenhurst (SW) 4E4
Brockholes (NT) 21F2/42D5
Brockley (SN) 40E3
Brockley Whins (NT) 28C5
Bromborough (ME) 20C4/45F5
Bromborough Rake (ME) 45F4
Bromley by Bow (LT) 40C3
Bromley Cross (NT) 20A2/24E2/45B1
Bromley North (SE) 5B4/40F2
Bromley South (SE) 5B4/40G2
Bromsgrove (CT) 9A4
Brondesbury (SL) 39B4
Brondesbury Park (SL) 39B4

Bronwydd Arms (Pres) 13G4
Brooklands (Metrolink) 20C1/20G1/45B3
Brookmans Park (FC) 11G2
Brookwood (SW) 5C1
Broome (GW) 14C1
Broomfleet (NT) 22E5
Broomhill (Pres) 36F3
Brora (SR) 36A4/38G5
Brough (TP) 22E4
Broughty Ferry (SR) 34E4
Broxbourne (FC) 11F3
Bruce Grove (LE) 40A4
Brundall (LE) 18F2
Brundall Gardens (LE) 18F2
Brunswick (ME) 20C4
Bruton (GW) 3C3
Bryn (NT) 20B3/24F3/45D3
Brynglas (Pres) 13B5
Brynhynod (Pres) 19F4
Buckenham (LE) 18F2
Buckfastleigh (Pres) 2D4
Buckhurst Hill (LT) 5A4
Buckley (AW) 20E4
Bucknell (AW) 14D1
Bugle (GW) 1D2
Builth Road (GW) 14E3
Bulwell (CT; NET) 16C4/41F4
Bulwell Forest (NET) 41F4
Bungalow (IoM) 23B3
Bures (LE) 12E5
Burgess Hill (SN) 5E3
Burley in Wharfedale (NT) 21C2
Burley Park (NT) 21D3, 42A3
Burnage (NT) 45A3
Burneside (TP) 27G1
Burnham (GW) 5B1/10G1
Burnham on Crouch (LE) 6A4/12G5
Burnley Barracks (NT) 24D1
Burnley Central (NT) 24D1
Burnley Manchester Road (NT) 24D1
Burnside (SR) 29C5/44D3
Burntisland (SR) 30A2
Burnt Oak (LT) 5A2
Burscough Bridge (NT) 20B4/24F3/45E1
Burscough Junction (NT) ...20B4/24F3/45E1
Bursledon (SW) 4E3
Burton Joyce (CT) 16C3
Burton on Trent (CT) 15E5
Bury (Metrolink) 20B1/20F1/45B1
Bury Bolton Street (Pres) ...20B1/24F1/45B1
Bury St Edmunds (LE) 12C5
Busby (SR) 29C5/44D2
Bush Hill Park (LE) 11G3
Bushey (SL) 5A2
Butlers Hill (NET) 41E4
Butlers Lane (CT) 15F5
Butlins Penychain (CT) 19F1
Butterley (Pres) 16C5/41E2
Buxted (SN) 5E4
Buxton (Norfolk; Pres) 18E3
Buxton (NT) 15A4
Byfleet & New Haw (SW) 5C1
Bynea (AW) 7B3

Cadoxton (AW) 8D4/43B5
Caergwrle (AW) 20E4
Caerphilly (AW) 8C4/43B3
Caersws (AW) 14C3
Caldicot (AW) 8B2/9F1
Caledonian Road & Barnsbury (SL) 40B5

Calstock (GW) 1C5
Cam & Dursley (GW) 9F2
Camberley (SW) 4B1
Camborne (GW) 1E5
Cambridge (LE) 11C3
Cambridge Heath (LE) 40C2
Camden Road (SL) 40B5
Cambuslang (SR) 29C5/44D3
Camelon (SR) 30B5
Canada Water (LT) 40D4
Canary Wharf (DLR) 40C3
Canley (CT) 10A5
Canning Town (SL; DLR) 40C2
Cannock (CT) 15E4
Canonbury (SL) 40B4
Canons Park (LT) 5A2
Canterbury East (SE) 6C3
Canterbury West (SE) 6C3
Cantley (LE) 18F2
Capel Bangor (Pres) 13B5
Capenhurst (ME) 20D4/45F5
Carbis Bay (GW) 1E4
Carbrook (SYS) 42G2
Cardenden (SR) 30A2
Cardiff Bay (AW) 43B5
Cardiff Central (AW) 8C4/43B4
Cardiff Queen Street (AW) 43B4
Cardonald (SR) 44F3
Cardross (SR) 29B3
Carfin (SR) 30C5/44A2
Cark (NT) 24B4
Carlisle (VT) 26C1
Carlton (CT) 16C3/41F5
Carluke (SR) 30D5
Carmarthen (AW) 7A2/13G4
Carmyle (SR) 29C5/44D3
Carnforth (TP) 24B3
Carnoustie (SR) 34E3
Carntyne (SR) 29C5/44D3
Carpenders Park (SL) 5A2
Carrbridge (SR) 36F4
Carrog (Pres) 19F5
Carrog (Pres) 20F5
Carshalton (SN) 5C3
Carshalton Beeches (SN) 5C3
Carstairs (SR) 30D4
Cartsdyke (SR) 29B3
Castle Bar Park (GW) 39C2
Castle Caereinion (Pres) 14B2
Castle Cary (GW) 3C3/8F1
Castle Hedingham (Pres) 11E5
Castleford (NT) 21E4/42B1
Castleton (NT) 20B1/24F1/45A1
Castleton Moor (NT) 28F3
Castletown (IoM) 23C2
Caterham (SN) 5C3
Catford (SE) 40E3
Catford Bridge (SE) 40E3
Cathays (AW) 43B4
Cathcart (SR) 29C5/44E3
Cattal (NT) 21C4
Causeland (GW) 1D4
Cefn-y-Bedd (AW) 20E4
Chadwell Heath (LE) 5A4
Chafford Hundred (CC) 5B5
Chalfont & Latimer (LT) 10F1
Chalkwell (CC) 6A4
Chapel-en-le-Frith (NT) 15A4
Chapeltown (NT) 21F3/42F2
Chapleton (GW) 7F3

Chappel & Wakes Colne (LE) 12E5
Charing (SE) .6C4
Charing Cross (Glasgow) (SR) 44E4
Charlbury (GW) 10D5
Charlton (SE) 5B4/40D2
Chartham (SE) 6C3
Chassen Road (NT) 45B3
Chatelherault (SR) 30C5/44B2
Chatham (SE) .6B5
Chathill (NT) 31E5
Cheadle Hulme (NT) 20C1/24G1/45A4
Cheam (SN) 5C3
Cheddington (SL) 10E1
Cheddleton (Pres) 15C4
Chelford (NT) 15A3/20D1/45B5
Chelmsford (LE) 11F5
Chelsfield (SE) 5C4
Cheltenham Spa (GW) 9D3
Chepstow (AW) 8B29F1
Cherry Tree (NT) 20A2/24E2
Chertsey (SW) 5B1
Chesham (LT) 10F1
Cheshunt (LE) 11G3
Chessington North (SW) 5C2
Chessington South (SW) 5C2
Chester (AW) 20D4
Chester le Street (NT) 27C5
Chester Road (CT) 15F5
Chesterfield (ML) 16A5/41C2
Chestfield & Swalecliffe (SE) 6B3
Chetnole (AW) 8E2
Chichester (SN) 4E1
Chigwell (LT) 5A4
Chilham (SE) 6C3
Chilworth (GW) 5D1
Chingford (LE) 11G3
Chinley (NT) 15A4
Chinnor (Pres) 10F2
Chippenham (GW) 3A4
Chipstead (SN) 5C3
Chirk (AW) .20F4
Chislehurst (SE) 5B4/40F2
Chiswick (SW) 39D3
Chiswick Park (LT) 39D3
Cholsey (GW) 10F4
Chorley (NT) 20A3/24E2/45D1
Chorleywood (LT) 5A1/10F1/11G1
Christchurch (SW) 4F5
Christs Hospital (SN) 5E2
Church & Oswaldtwistle (NT) 24D1
Church Fenton (NT) 21D4
Church Stretton (AW) 14B1/15F1
Churston (Pres) 2D3
Cilmeri (AW) 14E3
Cinderhill (NET) 41F4
City Hall (SYS) 41A2
Clacton (LE) 12F3
Clandon (SW) 5C1
Clapham (NT) 24B1
Clapham High Street (SN) 40E5
Clapham Junction (SW) 5B3/39E5
Clapham (N. Yorks) (NT) 24B1
Clapton (LE) 40B4
Clarbeston Road (AW) 13G1
Clarkston (SR) 29C5/44E2
Claverdon (CT) 9B5
Claygate (SW) 5C2
Clayton West (Pres) 21F3/42D3
Cleethorpes (TP) 22F2
Cleland (SR) 30C5/44A2

Clifton (NT) 20B1/24F1/45B2
Clifton Down (GW) 3A2/8C2/9G1
Clitheroe (NT) 24D1
Clock House (SE) 40F4
Clunderwen (AW) 13G2
Clydebank (SR) 29C4/44F4
Coatbridge (SR) 44B4
Coatbridge Sunnyside (SR) 44B4
Coatdyke (SR) 44B4
Cobham & Stoke d'Abernon (SW) 5C2
Codsall (CT) 15F3
Cogan (AW) 8C4/43B5
Colby (IoM) 23C2
Colchester (LE) 12E4
Colchester Town (LE) 12E4
Coleslogett Halt (Pres) 1D3
Colindale (LT) 5A2
Collingham (CT) 16B2
Collington (SN) 6F5
Colne (NT) .24D1
Coltishall (Pres) 18E3
Colwall (CT) .9C2
Colwyn Bay (AW) 19D4
Colyford (Pres) 2B1
Colyton (Pres) 2B1
Combe (GW) 10E5
Commondale (NT) 28F3
Congleton (NT) 15B3/20D1
Conisborough (NT) 21F4
Connel Ferry (SR) 32E4
Cononley (NT) 21C1
Consall (Pres) 15C4
Conwy (AW) 19D3
Cooden Beach (SN) 6F5
Cookham (GW) 5A1/10G2
Cooksbridge (SN) 5F4
Coombe (GW) 1D4
Coombe Lane (CTL) 5C3
Copplestone (GW) 2A4
Corbridge (NT) 27B3
Corfe Castle (Pres) 3G5
Corkerhill (SR) 44F3
Corkickle (NT) 26E4
Corpach (SR) 32C3
Corrour (SR) 32C1
Corwen (Pres) 19F5
Coryton (AW) 43B4
Coseley (CT) 13A1/15F3
Cosford (CT) 15F3
Cosham (SW) 4E2
Cottingham (NT) 22D3
Cottingley (NT) 21D3/41B3
Coulsdon South (SN) 5C3
Country Park Halt (Pres) 15G2
Coventry (VT) 10A5
Cowden (SN) .5D4
Cowdenbeath (SR) 30A3
Cownhayne (Pres) 2B1
Cradley Heath (CT) 15G4
Craigendoran (SR) 29B3
Cramlington (NT) 27B5
Cranmore (Pres) 3C3/8F1
Cranmore West (Pres) 3C3/8F1
Craven Arms (AW) 14C1
Crawley (SN) 5D3
Crayford (SE) 5B4
Crediton (GW) 2B2
Cressing (LE) 11F5
Cressington (ME) 20C4/24G4/45F4
Creswell (CT) 16A4/41B4

Crewe (VT) 15C2/20E2
Crewkerne (SW) 3E1
Crews Hill (FC) 11G2
Crianlarich (SR) 32F1
Criccieth (AW) 19F2
Cricket Inn Road (SYS) 42G2
Cricklade (Pres) 9F5
Cricklewood (FC) 5A3/39B4
Croesor Junction (Pres) 19F2
Croftfoot (SR) 44D3
Crofton Park (SE) 40E3
Cromer (LE) 18D3
Cromford (CT) 16B5/41D1
Crookston (SR) 29C4/44F3
Cross Gates (NT) 21D3/42A2
Crossharbour (DLR) 40D3
Crossflatts (NT) 21D2/42A5
Crosshill (SR) 44E3
Crossmyloof (SR) 29C5/44E3
Croston (NT) 20A3/24E3/45E1
Crouch Hill (SL) 40A5
Crowborough (SN) 5E5
Crowcombe Heathfield (Pres) 8F4
Crowhurst (SE) 6F5
Crowle (NT) 22F5
Crowthorne (GW) 4B1
Croy (SR) 30B5/44B5
Crumpsall (Metrolink) 20B1/20F1/45A2
Crystal Palace (SN) 5B3/40F4
Crystal Peaks (SYS) 41A3
Cuckoo's Nest (Pres) 42D3
Cuddington (NT) 15B2/20D2/45B5
Cuffley (FC) 11G2
Culham (GW) 10F4
Cullercoats (T&W) 28B5
Culrain (SR) 35A5
Cumbernauld (SR) 30B5/44B5
Cupar (SR) .34F4
Curriehill (SR) 30C3
Custom House (SL; DLR) 40C2
Cutty Sark (DLR) 40D3
Cuxton (SE) .6B5
Cwmbach (AW) 8B5/43D2
Cwmbran (AW) 8B3/43A3
Cwmdwyfran (Pres) 13G4
Cyfronydd (Pres) 14C2
Cynghordy (AW) 14F5
Cynwl Elfed (Pres) 13G4
Cyprus (DLR) 40C1

Dagenham Dock (CC) 5A4
Daisy Hill (NT) 20B2/24F2/45C2
Dalgety Bay (SR) 30B3
Dalmally (SR) 32F2
Dalmarnock (SR) 44D3
Dalmeny (SR) 30B3
Dalmuir (SR) 29C4/44G5
Dalreoch (SR) 29B3
Dalry (SR) .29D3
Dalston (NT) 26C1
Dalston Kingsland (SL) 40B4
Dalton (NT) .24B5
Dalwhinnie (SR) 33B2
Damems (Pres) 21D1
Danby (NT) .28F3
Danescourt (AW) 43B4
Danzey (CT) .9A5
Darley Dale (Pres) 16B5/41D1
Darlington (GR) 28F5
Darnall (NT) 16A5/21G4/41A2/42G1

Darsham (LE) 12B2
Dartford (SE) 5B5
Dartmouth Street (Midland Metro) 13B2
Darton (NT) 21F3/42D3
Darwen (NT) 20A2/24E2
Datchet (SW) 5B1/10G1
Davenport (NT) 215A3/0C1/21G1/45A4
David Lane (NET) 41F4
Dawlish (GW) 2C3
Dawlish Warren (GW) 2C3
Dduallt (Pres) 19F3
Deal (SE) 6C1
Dean (GW) 4D5
Dean Lane (NT) 45A3
Deansgate (NT) 45B3
Debden (LT) 5A4/11G3
Deganwy (AW) 19C3
Deighton (NT) 21E242C4
Delamere (NT) 15B1/20D3
Denby Dale (NT) 21F3/42D3
Denham (CH) 5A1/10G1
Denham Golf Club (CH) 5A1/10G1
Denmark Hill (SE) 40D4
Dent (NT) 24A1
Denton (NT) 20C1/21G1/45A3
Deptford (SE) 5D3
Deptford Bridge (DLR) 40D3
Derby (ML) 16D5/41G2
Derby Road (LE) 12D3
Dereham (Pres) 18E4
Derker (NT) 21F1
Devonport (NT) 1D5
Devons Road (DLR) 40C3
Dewsbury (TP) 21E3/42C3
Didcot Parkway (GW) 10F4
Digby & Sowton (GW) 2B3
Dilton Marsh (GW) 3B4
Dinas (AW) 8B5/43D3
Dinas Powys (AW) 8D4/43B5
Dingle Road (AW) 8C4/43B5
Dingwall (SR) 35D5
Dinsdale (NT) 28F5
Dinting (NT) 21G1
Disley (NT) 15A4
Diss (LE) 12B4
Dockyard (GW) 1D5
Dodworth (NT) 21F3/42E3
Dolau (AW) 14D3
Doleham (SN) 6F5
Dolgarrog (AW) 19D3
Dolgoch Falls (Pres) 13B5
Dollis Hill (LT) 39B4
Dolwyddelen (AW) 19E3
Dolygaer (Pres) 8A5/43C1
Doncaster (GR) 21F5
Donetsk Way (SYS) 41A2
Doniford Beach Halt (Pres) 8E5
Dorchester South (SW) 3F3
Dorchester West (GW) 3F3
Dore (NT) 16A5/41A1
Dorking (SN) 5C2
Dorking (Deepdene) (GW) 5C2
Dorking West (GW) 5C2
Dormans (SN) 5D4
Dorridge (CT) 9A5
Douglas (IoM) 23C3
Dove Holes (NT) 15A4
Dover Priory (SE) 6D2
Dovercourt (LE) 12E3
Dovey Junction (AW) 14B5

Downham Market (FC) 17F4
Drayton Green (GW) 39C2
Drayton Park (FC) 40B5
Drem (SR) 30B1
Driffield (NT) 22C4
Drigg (NT) 26G3
Droitwich Spa (CT) 9B3
Dronfield (NT) 16A5/41B2
Drumchapel (SR) 44F4
Drumfrochar (SR) 29B3
Drumgelloch (SR) 30C5/44A4
Drumry (SR) 44F4
Duddeston (CT) 13C4
Dudley Port (CT) 13B2/15G4
Dudley Street,
    Guns Village (Midland Metro) 13B2
Duffield (CT) 16C5/41F2
Dufftown (Pres) 36E1
Duirinish (SR) 35F1
Duke Street (SR) 44D4
Dullingham (LE) 11C5
Dumbarton Central (SR) 29B3
Dumbarton East (SR) 29B3
Dumbreck (SR) 44E3
Dumfries (SR) 26B4
Dumpton Park (SE) 6B1
Dunbar (GR) 31B1
Dunblane (SR) 30A5/33G3
Dunbridge (GW) 4D4
Duncraig (SR) 35E1
Dundee (Tay Bridge) (SR) 34E4
Dundonald Road (CTL) 39F4
Dunfermline Queen Margaret (SR) 30A3
Dunfermline Town (SR) 30A3
Dungeness (Pres) 6E3
Dunkeld & Birnam (SR) 33D4
Dunlop (SR) 29D4
Dunrobin Castle (SR) 36A4/38G5
Dunster (Pres) 8E5
Dunston (NT) 28B2
Dunton Green (SE) 5C4
Durham (GR) 27D5
Durrington on Sea (SN) 5F2
Dyce (SR) 37F4
Dyffryn Ardudwy (AW) 19G2
Dymchurch (Pres) 6E3

Eaglescliffe (NT) 28E5
Ealing Broadway (GW) 5B2/39C2
Ealing Common (LT) 39C3
Eardington (Pres) 15G2
Earlestown (NT) 20C3/24G2/45D3
Earley (SW) 4A2
Earls Court (LT) 39D5
Earlsfield (SW) 39E5
Earlswood (Surrey) (SN) 5D3
Earlswood (West Midlands) (CT) 9A5
East Acton (LT) 39C4
East Boldon (T&W) 28C5
East Croydon (SN) 5C3
East Didsbury (NT) 45A4
East Dulwich (SN) 40E4
East Farleigh (SE) 6Cf
East Finchley (LT) 5A3
East Garforth (NT) 21D4/42A1
East Grinstead (SN) 5D4
East Ham (LT) 40B2
East India (DLR) 40C3
East Kilbride (SR) 29D5/44D1
East Malling (SE) 6C5

East Putney (LT) 39E4
East Tilbury (CC) 5B5
East Worthing (SN) 5F2
Eastbourne (SN) 5G5
Eastbrook (AW) 43B5
Eastcote (LT) 39B1
Easterhouse (SR) 44C4
Eastgate (Pres) 27D3
Eastham Rake (ME) 45F5
Eastleigh (SW) 4D3
Eastrington (NT) 22D5
Ebbw Vale (AW; proposed) 8A4/43B1
Eccles (NT) 45B3
Eccles Road (CT) 12A4/18G4
Eccleston Park (NT) 20C3/24G3/45E3
Edale (NT) 15A5
Eden Park (SE) 5B3//40G3
Edenbridge (SE) 5D4
Edenbridge Town (SN) 5D4
Edinburgh Park (SR) 30B3
Edge Hill (NT) 20C4/24G4/45F4
Edgware (LT) 5A2
Edgware Road (LT) 39C5
Edinburgh (Waverley) (NW) 30B2
Edinburgh Park (SR) 30B3
Edmonton Green (LE) 5A3
Effingham Junction (SW) 5C2
Eggesford (GW) 2A5/7G4
Egham (SW) 5B1
Egton (NT) 28F2
Elephant & Castle (FC) 40D5
Elgin (SR) 36C2
Ellerson Road (DLR) 40D3
Ellesmere Port (ME) 20D4/45F5
Elmers End (SE; CTL) 5B3/40F4
Elmstead Woods (SE) 40F2
Elmswell (LE) 12C4
Elsecar (NT) 21F3/42E2
Elsenham (LE) 11E4
Elstree & Borehamwood (FC) 11G2
Eltham (SE) 5B4/40E1
Elton & Orston (CT) 16C2
Elverson Road (DLR); 40D3
Ely (LE) 11B4
Embsay (Pres) 21C1
Emerson Park (LE) 5A5
Emsworth (SN) 4E2
Enfield Chase (FC) 11G2
Enfield Lock (LE) 11G3
Enfield Town (LE) 11G2
Entwistle (NT) 20A2/24E2/45B1
Epping (LT) 11G3
Epsom (SW) 5C2
Epsom Downs (SN) 5C3
Erdington (CT) 15F5
Eridge (SN) 5D5
Erith (SE) 5B4
Esher (SW) 5B2/39G1
Eskdale (Pres) 26F2
Essex Road (FC) 40B5
Etchingham (SE) 6E5
Euston Square (LT) 40D5
Euxton Balshaw Lane (NT) 24E3
Evesham (GW) 9C4
Ewell East (SN) 5C3
Ewell West (SW) 5C3
Exeter Central (GW) 2B3
Exeter St Davids (GW) 2B3
Exeter St Thomas (GW) 2C3
Exhibition Centre (SR) 44E4

Exmouth (GW) 2C3
Exton (GW) 2B3
Eynsford (SE) 5C5

Failsworth (NT) 20B1/45A2
Fairbourne (AW) 13A5
Fairfield (NT) 45A3
Fairlie (SR) 29D2
Fairlop (LT) 5A4/40A1
Fairwater (AW) 43B4
Falconwood (SE) 40E1
Falkirk Grahamston (SR) 30B4
Falkirk High (SR) 30B4
Falls of Cruachan (SR) 32F3
Falmer (SN) 5F3
Falmouth Docks (GW) 1F1
Falmouth Town (GW) 1F1
Fambridge (LE) 12G5
Fareham (SW) 4E3
Farnborough (Main) (SW) 4B1
Farnborough North (GW) 4B1
Farncombe (SW) 5D1
Farnham (SW) 4C1
Farningham Road (SE) 5B5
Farringdon (LT) 40D5
Farnworth (NT) 20B2/24F1/45B2
Fauldhouse (SR) 30C4
Faversham (SE) 6C3
Fawdon (T&W) 27B5
Faygate (SN) 5D3
Fazackerley (ME) 20B4/24F4/45F3
Fearn (SR) 36B4
Featherstone (NT) 21E4/42C1
Felixstowe (LE) 12E2
Fellgate (T&W) 28C5
Felling (T&W) 28A1
Feltham (SW) 5B2
Feniton (SW) 2B2
Fenny Stratford (SL) 10D2
Fernhill (AW) 8B5/43C2
Ferriby (NT) 22E4
Ferry Meadows (Pres) 11A1/17F1
Ferryside (AW) 7A2
Ffairfach (AW) 13G5
Fieldway (CTL) 5C4
Filey (NT) 22A3
Filton Abbey Wood (GW) 3A2/8C1/9G1
Finchley Central (LT) 5A3
Finchley Road & Frognal (SL) 39B2
Finsbury Park (FC) 5A3/40B5
Finghall (Pres) 27G5
Finstock (GW) 10E5
Fishbourne (SN) 4E1
Fishergate (SN) 5F3
Fisherground (Pres) 26F2
Fishguard Harbour (AW) 13F1
Fiskerton (CT) 16C3
Fitzwilliam (NT) 21E4/42D1
Five Ways (CT) 13C3
Fleet (SW) .4B1
Flimby (NT) 26D3
Flint (AW) 20D5
Flitwick (FC) 10D1/11E1
Flixton (NT) 20C2/24G1/45B3
Flowery Field (NT) 21G1
Folkestone Central (SE) 6D2
Folkestone West (SE) 6D2
Ford (SN) .5F1
Forest Gate (LE) 40B2
Forest Hill (SN) 40E4

Formby (ME) 20B4/24F4/45G2
Forres (SR) 36D3
Forsinard (SR) 38E5
Fort Matilda (SR) 29B3
Fort William (SR) 32C3
Four Oaks (CT) 15F5
Foxfield (NT) 24A5
Foxton (FC) 11D3
Frant (SE) .5D5
Fratton (SW) 4E2
Freshfield (ME) 20B4/24F4/45G2
Freshford (GW) 3B4
Frimley (SW) 4B1/5C1
Frinton on Sea (LE) 12E3
Frizinghall (NT) 21D2/42A5
Frodsham (AW) 15A1/20D3/45D5
Frome (GW) 3C3
Frosterley (Pres) 27D4
Fulham Broadway (LT) 39D4
Fulwell (SW) 5B2/39F1
Furness Vale (NT) 15A4
Furze Platt (GW) 10G2

Gainsborough Central (NT) 16A2
Gainsborough Lea Road (CT) 22G5
Gallions Reach (DLR) 40C1
Garelochhead(SR) 29A3
Garforth (NT) 21D4/42A1
Gargrave (NT) 21C1
Garrowhill . . . . (SR)44C3
Garscadden (SR) 29C4/44F4
Garsdale (NT) 24A1/27G2
Garston (Herts) (SL) 11G1
Garswood (NT) 20B3/24F3/45D3
Gartcosh (SR 44C4
Garth (Mid-Glamorgan) (AW) 7B5/43E3
Garth (Powys) (AW) 14E4
Garve (SR) 35D4
Gateshead (T&W) 28A1
Gateshead Stadium (T&W) 28A1
Gathurst (NT) 20B3/24F3/45D2
Gatley (NT) 45A4
Gatwick Airport (NW) 5D3
Georgemas Junction (SR) 38C3
Gerrards Cross (CH) 5A1/10F1
Gidea Park (LE) 5A4
Giffnock (SR) 29C5/44E2
Giggleswick (NT) 24B1
Gilberdyke (NT) 22E5
Gilfach Dhu (Pres) 19D2
Gilfach Fargoed (AW) 8B4/43B2
Gillingham (Dorset) (SW) 3D4
Gillingham (Kent) (SE) 6B5
Gilslochill (SR) 44E4
Gipsy Hill (SN) 40F4
Girvan (SR) 29G2
Glaisdale (NT) 28F2
Glan Conwy (AW) 19D4
Glan Llyn Halt (Pres) 19F4
Glasgow Central (NW) 29C5/44E4
Glasgow Queen Street (SR) 29C5/44E4
Glasshoughton (NT) 42C1
Glazebrook (NT) 20C2/24G2/45C3
Gleadless Townend (SYS) 41A2
Gleneagles (SR) 33F4
Glenfinnan (SR) 32B4
Glengarnock (SR) 29D3
Glenrothes with Thornton (SR) 30A2
Glossop (NT) 21G1
Gloucester (GW) 9D3

Gloucester Road (LT) 39D5
Glynde (SN) 5F4
Glyndyfrdwy (Pres) 20F5
Goathland (Pres) 28F2
Gobowen (AW) 20F4
Godalming (SW) 5D1
Godley (NT) 21G1
Godstone (SE) 5D3
Golders Green (LT) 5A3
Gold Hawk Road (LT) 39D4
Goldthorpe (NT) 21F4/42E1
Golf Street (SR) 34E3
Golspie (SR) 36A4
Gomshall (GW) 5D2
Goodmayes (LE) 5A4
Goodrington Sands (Pres) 2D3
Goole (NT) 22E5
Goostrey (NT) 15B3/20D1
Gordon Hill (FC) 11G2
Goring & Streatley (GW) 10G3
Goring by Sea (SN) 5F2
Gorsey Bank (Pres) 16C5/41E1
Gorton (NT) 45A3
Gospel Oak (SL) 39B5
Gourock (SR) 29B3
Gowerton (AW) 7B2
Goxhill (NT) 22E3
Grange Park (FC) 11G2
Grange-over-Sands (TP) 24B3
Grangetown (AW) 8C4/43B4
Grantham (GR) 16D1
Granton on Spey (Pres) 36F3
Granville Road (SYS) 42G2
Grateley (SW) 4C5
Gravel Hill (CTL) 5C3
Gravelly Hill (CT) 15G5
Gravesend (SE) 5B5
Grays (CC) .5B5
Great Ayrton (NT) 28F4
Great Bentley (LE) 12E4
Great Chesterford (LE) 11D4
Great Coates (NT) 22F2
Great Malvern (CT) 9C3
Great Missenden (CH) 10F2
Great Portland Street (LT) 39C5
Great Yarmouth (LE) 18F1
Green Lane (ME) 45F4
Green Road (NT) 24A5
Greenbank (NT) 15A2/20D2/45C5
Greenfaulds (SR) 30B5/44B5
Greenfield (NT) 21F1
Greenford (LT) 5A2/39B1
Greenhithe for Bluewater (SE) 5B5
Greenock Central (SR) 29B3
Greenock West (SR) 29B3
Greenwich (SE; CTL) 5B4/40D3
Gretna Green (SR) 26B1
Gretton Meadow (Pres) 9D4
Grimsby Docks (NT) 22F2
Grimsby Town (TP) 22F2
Grindleford (NT) 16A5/41B1
Groombridge (Pres) 5D4
Grosmont (NT) 28F2
Grove Park (SE) 40E2
Guide Bridge (NT) 21F1
Guildford (SW) 5C1
Guiseley (NT) 21D2
Gunnersbury (SL) 39D3
Gunnislake (GW) 1C5
Gunton (LE) 18D3

Gwersyllt (AW) 20E4
Gypsy Lane (NT) 28E4

Habrough (NT) .22F3
Hackbridge (SN) 39G5
Hackenthorpe (SYS) 41A2
Hackney Central (SL) 40B3
Hackney Downs (LE) 5A3/40B4
Hackney Wick (SL) 40B3
Halfway (SYS) 16A4/41A3
Hamble (SW) 4E3
Haddenham & Thame Parkway (CH) . . .10E3
Haddiscoe (LE) 12A2/18F1
Hadfield (NT) 21G1
Hadley Wood (FC) 11G2
Hadrian Road (T&W) 28B5
Hag Fold (NT) 20B2/24F2/45C2
Hagley (CT) 9A3
Hairmyres (SR) 29D5/44D1
Hale (NT) 15A3/20C1/24G1/45B4
Halesworth (LE) 12B2
Halewood (NT) 15A1/20C3/24G3/45E4
Halifax (NT) 21E2/42B5
Hall Green (CT) 9A5/15G5
Hall i' th' Wood (NT) 20B2/24F2/45B1
Hall Road (ME) 20B4/24F4/45F2
Halling (SE) 6C5
Haltwhistle (NT) 27B2
Ham Street (SN) 6D4
Hamilton Central (SR) 30C5/44B2
Hamilton Square (Birkenhead) (ME) . . .45F4
Hamilton West (SR) 44B2
Hammersmith (LT) 39D4
Hammerton (NT) 21C4
Hampden Park (SN) 5F5
Hampstead Heath (SL) 39B5
Hampton (SW) 5B2/39F1
Hampton Court (SW) 5B2/39G2
Hampton in Arden (CT) 15G5
Hampton Loade (Pres) 15G2
Hampton Wick (SW) 39F2
Hamstead (CT) 13B3/15F4
Hamworthy (SW) 3F4
Hanborough (GW) 10E4
Handforth (NT) 15A3/20C1/45A4
Handsworth Booth Street
    (Midland Metro) 13B3
Hanwell (GW) 5B2/39C2
Hapton (NT) 24D1
Harlech (AW) .19F2
Harlesden (SL) 39B3
Harling Road (LE) 12A4/18G4
Harlington (FC) 10D1/11E1
Harlow Mill (LE) 11F3
Harlow Town (LE) 11F3
Harman's Cross (Pres) 3G5
Harold Wood (LE) 5A5
Harpenden (FC) 11F1
Harrietsham (SE) 6C4
Harringay (FC) 40A5
Harringay Green Lanes (SL) 40A5
Harrington (NT) 26E3
Harrington Road (CTL) 40G4
Harrogate (NT) 21C3
Harrow & Wealdstone (SL) 39A2
Harrow (Sudbury Hill) (CH) 39B2
Harrow on the Hill (LT) 5A2/39A2
Hartford (CT) 15B2/20D2/45C5
Hartlebury (CT) 9A3
Hartlepool (NT) 28D4

Hartwood (SR) 30C5
Harwich International (LE) 12E3
Harwich Town (LE) 12E3
Haslemere (SW) 4C1/5D1
Hassocks (SN) .5F3
Hastings (SE) 6F5
Hatch End (SL) 5A2
Hatfield (FC) .11F2
Hatfield & Stainforth (NT) 21F5
Hatfield Peverel (LE) 11F5
Hathersage (NT) 15A5
Hattersley (NT) 21G1
Hatton (CT) 9B5
Hatton Cross (LT) 5B2
Havant (SW) 4E2
Haven Street (Pres) 4F3
Havenhouse (CT) 17B4
Haverfordwest (AW) 7C2
Haverthwaite (Pres) 24A4
Hawarden (AW) 20D4
Hawarden Bridge (AW) 19D4
Hawkhead (SR) 44F3
Haworth (Pres) 21D1
Haydon Bridge (NT) 27B3
Haydons Road (FC) 39F5
Hayes & Harlington (GW) 5B2
Hayes (LE) 5C4/40G2
Hayle (GW) 1E4
Haymarket (SR) 30B2
Haywards Heath (SN) 5E3
Hazel Grove (NT) 15A3/20C1/45A4
Headcorn (SE) 6D5
Headingley (NT) 21D3/42A3
Headstone Lane (SL) 39A1
Heald Green (NT) . . .15A3/20C1/24G1/45A4
Healing (NT) .22F2
Heath (High Level) (AW) 43B4
Heath (Low Level) (AW) 43B4
Heathrow London Airport (HX) 5B2
Heaton Chapel (NT) 45A3
Heaton Park (Metrolink) 20B1/45B2
Hebburn (T&W) 28B5
Hebden Bridge (NT) 21E1
Heckington (CT) 17C2
Hedge End (SW) 4E3
Hednesford (CT) 15E4
Heighington (NT) 27E5
Helensburgh Central (SR) 29B3
Helensburgh Upper (SR) 29B3
Hellifield (NT) 24C1
Helmsdale (SR) 38F4
Helsby (AW) 15A1/20D3/45E5
Hemel Hempstead (SL) 10E1/11F1
Hendon (FC) 5A3/39A4
Hendon Central (LT) 5A3
Hengoed (AW) 8B4/43B3
Heniarth (Pres) 14C2
Henley on Thames (GW) 10G2
Henley-in-Arden (CT) 9B5
Henllan (Pres) 13F4
Hensall (NT) .21E5
Herdings Leighton Road (SYS) 41A2
Herdings Park (SYS) 16A5/41A2
Hereford (AW) 9C1
Herne Bay (SE) 6B2
Herne Hill (SE) 40E5
Heron Quays (DLR) 40C3
Hersham (SW) 5C2
Herston Halt (Pres) 3G5
Hertford East (LE) 11F2

Hertford North (FC) 1F2
Hessle (NT) 22E4
Heswall (NT) 20C4/45F4
Hever (SN) 5D4
Heworth (NT) 28A1
Hexham (NT) .27B3
Heyford (GW) 10D4
Heysham Port (NT) 24C4
Heywood (Pres) 20B1/24F1/45A2
High Barnet (LT) 5A3/11G2
High Brooms (SE) 5D5
High Rocks Halt (Pres) 5D5
High Street (SR) 44D4
High Wycombe (CH) 10F2
Higham (SE) .6B5
Highams Park (LE) 5A4
Highbridge & Burnham on Sea (GW) 3B1/8E3
Highbury & Islington (LT) 40B5
Highbury Vale (NET) 41F4
Highley (Pres) 9A2/15G2
High Street Kensington (LT) 39D5
Hightown (ME) 20B4/24F4/45F2
Hildenborough (SE) 5D5
Hillfoot (SR) 29B4/44E5
Hillingdon (LT) 5A2
Hillington East (SR) 44F3
Hillington West (SR) 44F3
Hillsborough (SYS) 42G2
Hillsborough Park (SYS) 42G2
Hillside (ME) 20A4/24E4/45F1
Hilsea (SN) 4E2
Hinchley Wood (SW) 5C2
Hinckley (CT) 16F4
Hindley (NT) 20B2/24F2/45C2
Hinton Admiral (SW) 4F5
Hitchin (FC) .11E2
Hither Green (SE) 40E3
Hockley (LE) .6A5
Hollingbourne (SE) 6C5
Hollinsend (SYS) 41A2
Hollinwood (NT) 20B1/45A2
Holmes Chapel (NT) 15B3/20D1
Holmwood (SN) 5D2
Holt (Pres) 18D4
Holton Heath (SW) 3F4
Holyhead (AW) 19B1
Holytown (SR) 30C5/44A3
Holywell Halt (Pres) 21C1
Homerton (SL) 40B3
Honeybourne (GW) 9C5
Honiton (SW) 2A2
Honley (NT) 21F2/42D5
Honor Oak Park (SN) 40E4
Hook (SW) 4B2
Hooton (ME) 20D4/45F5
Hope (Derbyshire) (AW) 15A5
Hope (Flint) (NT) 20E4
Hopton Heath (AW) 14D1
Horley (SN) 5D3
Hornbeam Park (NT) 21C3
Hornsey (FC) .40A5
Horsforth (NT) 21D3/42A3
Horsham (SN) 5E2
Horsley (SW) .5C2
Horsted Keynes (Pres) 5E3
Horton in Ribblesdale (NT) 24B1
Horwich Parkway (NT) 20B2/24F2/45C2
Hoscar (NT) 20B3/24F3/45E1
Hough Green (NT) . . .15A1/20C3/24G3/45E4
Hounslow (SW) 5B239E1

Hounslow Central (LT) 39D1
Hounslow East (LT) 39D1
Hounslow West (LT) 39D1
Hove (SN) 5F3
Hoveton & Wroxham (LE) 18E2
How Wood (SL) 11G1
Howden (NT) 22E5
Howdon (T&W) 28B5
Hoylake (ME) 20C5/24G5
Hubberts Bridge (CT) 17C2
Hucknall (CT; NET) 16C4/41E4
Huddersfield (TP) 21E2/42C5
Hull (TP) 22E3
Humphrey Park (NT) 45B3
Huncoat (NT) 24D1
Hungerford (GW) 4A4
Hunmanby (NT) 22B3
Huntingdon (FC) 11B2
Huntly (SR) 37E1
Hunts Cross (ME) 20C3/24G3/45E4
Hurst Green (SN) 5C4
Hutton Cranswick (NT) 22C4
Huyton (NT) 20C3/24G3/45E4
Hyde Central (NT) 40E4
Hyde North (NT) 21G1
Hyde Park (SYS) 42G2
Hykeham (CT) .16B1
Hyndland (SR) .44E4
Hyson Green Market (NET) 41F4
Hythe (LE) 12E4

IBM (SR) 29B2
Ickenham (LT) 5A2
Ifield (SN) 5D3
Ilford (LE) 5A4/40B1
Ilkley (NT) 21C2
Imperial Wharf (SL) 39D5
Ince (NT) 20B3/24F2/45D2
Ince & Elton (NT) 15A1/20D3/45E5
Infirmary Road (SYS) 41A2/42G2
Ingatestone (LE) 11G4
Ingrow (Pres) 21D1
Insch (SR) 37E2
Invergordon (SR) 36C5
Invergowrie (SR) 34E5
Inverkeithing (SR) 30B3
Inverkip (SR) 29C2
Inverness (SR) .36E5
Invershin (SR) .35A5
Inverurie (SR) .37F3
Ipswich (LE) 12D4
Irlam (NT) 20C2/24G2/45C3
Irton Road (Pres) 26F3
Irvine (SR) 29E3
Irwell Vale (Pres) 20A1/24E1
Isfield (Pres) 5F4
Island Gardens (DLR) 40D3
Isleworth (SW) 5B2/39D2
Islip (GW) 10E4
Iver (GW) 5B1
Ivybridge (GW) 2D5

Jarrow (T&W) .28B5
Jefferstone Lane (Pres) 6E3
Jesmond (T&W) 28A1
Jesmond (T&W) 27B5
Jesmond (T&W) 27B5
Jewellery Quarter (CT) 13C3
Johnston (AW) .7C1
Johnstone (SR) .29C4

Jordanhill (SR) .44E4

Kearsley (NT) 20B2/24F1/45B2
Kearsney (SE) 6D2
Keighley (NT) .21D1
Keith (SR) 37D1
Kelling Heath Halt (Pres) 18D4
Kelvedon (LE) .12F5
Kelvindale (SR) 44E4
Kemble (GW) 9F4
Kempston Hardwick (SL) 10C1
Kempton Park (SW) 39F1
Kemsing (SE) 5C5
Kemsley (SE) 6B4
Kendal (TP) 24A3/27G1
Kenley (SN) 5C3
Kennett (LE) 11C5
Kennishead (SR) 44E3
Kensal Green (SL) 39B4
Kensal Rise (SL) 39B4
Kensington Olympia (SL) 5B3/39D4
Kent House (SE) 40F4
Kentish Town (FC) 40B5
Kentish Town West (SL) 40B5
Kenton (SL) 39A2
Kents Bank (SL) 24B4
Kettering (ML) 10A2
Kew Bridge (SW) 39D3
Kew Gardens (SL) 39D3
Keyham (GW) .1D5
Keynsham (GW) 3A3/8D1
Kidbrooke (SE) 40E2
Kidderminster (CT) 9A3
Kidsgrove (CT) 15C3/20E1
Kidwelly (AW) .7A2
Kilburn (LT) 39B4
Kilburn High Road (SL) 39B5
Kildale (NT) 28F3
Kildonan (SR) .38F5
Kilgetty (AW) .7D3
Kilmarnock (SR) 29E4
Kilmaurs (SR) .29E4
Kilpatrick (SR) 29B4/44G5
Kilwinning (SR) 29D3
Kimberley Park (Pres) 18F4
Kinbrace (SR) .38E5
King George V (DLR) 40C1
King Henry's Drive (CTL) 5C4
Kingham (GW) 9D5
Kinghorn (SR) .30A2
Kings Langley (SL) 11G1
Kings Lynn (FC) 17E4
Kings Norton (CT) 9A4
Kings Nympton (GW) 7G4
Kings Park (SR) 44D3
Kings Sutton (CH) 10C4
Kingsbury (LT) 39A3
Kingsknowe (SR) 30C2
Kingsley & Froghall (Pres) 15C4
Kingston (SW) 5B2/39F2
Kingswear (Pres) 2D3
Kingswood (SN) 5C3
Kingussie (SR) .33A2
Kinneil (Pres) 30B4
Kintbury (GW) .4A4
Kirby Cross (LE) 12E3
Kirk Sandall (NT) 21F5
Kirkby (ME) 20B4/24F3/45E3
Kirkby in Ashfield (CT) 16C4/41E4
Kirkby in Furness (NT) 24A5

Kirkby Stephen (NT) 27F2
Kirkcaldy (SR) .30A2
Kirkconnel (SR) 30F5
Kirkdale (ME) .45F3
Kirkham & Wesham (NT) 24D3
Kirkhill (SR) 29C5/44D2
Kirknewton (SR) 30C3
Kirkwood (SR) .44B3
Kirton Lindsey (NT) 22F4
Kiveton Bridge (NT) 16A4/41A4
Kiveton Park (NT) 16A4/41A4
Knaresborough (NT) 21C3
Knebworth (FC) 11E2
Knighton (AW) 14D2
Knockholt (SE) .5C4
Knottingley (NT) 21E4
Knucklas (AW) 14D2
Knutsford (NT) 15A2/20D2/45B5
Kyle of Lochalsh (SR) 35F1

Ladbroke Grove (LT) 39C4
Ladybank (SR) .34F5
Ladywell (SE) .40E3
Laindon (CC) 5A5
Lairg (SR) 35A5
Lake (IL) 4F3
Lakenheath (LE) 11A5/17G5
Lamphey (AW) .7D2
Lanark (SR) 30D4
Lancaster (VT) .24C3
Lancing (SN) 5F2
Landywood (CT) 15E4
Langbank (SR) .29B3
Langho (NT) 24D2
Langley (GW) 5B1/10G1
Langley Green (CT) 13C2/15G4
Langley Mill (CT) 16C4/41F3
Langsett/Primrose View (SYS) 42G2
Langside (SR) .44E3
Langwathby (NT) 27D1
Langwith-Whaley Thorns (CT) . . .16B4/41C4
Lapford (SR) 2A4
Lapworth (CH) .9A5
Larbert (SR) 30B5
Largs (SR) 29C2
Larkhall (SR) 30D5/44B1
Latimer Road (LT) 39C4
Lawrence Hill (GW) 3A2
Laxey (IoM) 23B3
Layton (NT) 24D4
Lazonby & Kirkoswald (NT) 27D1
Lea Green (NT) 20C3/24G3/45D3
Lea Hall (CT) 15G5
Leagrave (FC) 10D1/11E1
Lealhom (NT) .28F3
Leamington Spa (CH) 10B5
Leasowe (ME) 20C5/24G5
Leatherhead (SN) 5C2
Ledbury (CT) 9C2
Lee (SE) 5B4/40E2
Leeds (NW) 21D3/42A2
Leeming Bar (Pres) 28G5
Leicester (ML) .16F3
Leicester North (Pres) 16E4
Leigh (Kent) (SE) 5D5
Leigh on Sea (CC) 6A5
Leighton Buzzard (SL) 10D1
Lelant (GW) 1E4
Lelant Saltings (GW) 1E4
Lenham (SE) 6C4

Lenzie (SR) 29B5/44D5
Leominster (AW) 9B1
Leppings Lane (SYS) 42G2
Letchworth Garden City (FC) 11D2
Leuchars (SR) 34F4
Levenshulme (NT) 20C1/24G1/45A3
Levisham (Pres) 22A5/28G2
Lewes (SN) 5F4
Lewisham (SE; DLR) 40E3
Leyburn (Pres) 27G4
Leyland (NT) 20A3/24E3
Leyton (LT) .40B3
Leyton Midland Road (SL) 40B3
Leytonstone (LT) 5A4/40A2
Leytonstone High Road (SL) 40B2
Lichfield City (CT) 15E5
Lichfield Trent Valley (CT) E5
Lidlington (SL) 10C1
Limehouse (CC; DLR) 40C3
Lincoln (CT) 16B1/17B1
Lingfield (SN) 5D4
Lingwood (LE) 18F2
Linlithgow (SR) 30B3
Liphook (SW) 4D1
Liskeard (GW) 1D4
Liss (SW) 4D1
Lisvane & Thornhill (AW) 43B4
Little Kimble (CH) 10E2
Little Sutton (ME) 20D4/45F5
Littleborough (NT) 21E1
Littlehampton (SN) 5G1
Littlehaven (SN) 5E2
Littleport (FC) 11A4/17G4
Liverpool Central (ME) 20C4/24G4/45F3
Liverpool James Street (ME) 45F3
Liverpool Lime Street (NW) 20C4/24G4/45F3
Liverpool Moorfields (ME) 45F3
Liverpool South Parkway (ME) 45E4
Livingston North (SR) 30C4
Livingston South (SR) 30C3
Llanaber (AW) 13A5
Llanbadarn (Pres) 13C5
Llanbedr (AW) 19G2
Llanbister Road (AW) 14D2
Llanbradach (AW) 8B4/43B3
Llandaf (AW) 8C4/43B4
Llandanwg (AW) 19G2
Llandecwyn (AW) 19F2
Llandeilo (AW) 13G5
Llandovery (AW) 14F5
Llandrindod Wells (AW) 14E3
Llandudno (AW) 19C3
Llandudno Junction (AW) 19D3
Llandybie (AW) 7A3/43G1
Llanelli (AW) 7B3
Llanfair Caereinion (Pres) 14C2
Llanfair PG (AW) 19D2
Llanfairfechan (AW) 19D3
Llangadog (AW) 14G5
Llangammarch (AW) 14E4
Llangennech (AW) 7B3
Llangollen (Pres) 20F5
Llangynllu (AW) 14D2
Llangywair (Pres) 19F4
Llanishen (AW) 8C4/43B4
Llanrwst (AT) 19E4
Llansamlet (AW) 7B4/43F2
Llantwit Major (AW) 8D5/43D5
Llanuwchllyn (Pres) 19G4
Llanwrda (AW) 14F5

Llanwrtyd (AW) 14E4
Lloyd Park (CTL) 5C3
Llwyfan Cerrig (Pres) 13G4
Llwyngwril (AW) 13A5
Llwynpia (AW) 8B5/43D3
Loch Awe (SR) 32F2
Loch Eil Outward Bound (SR) 32C3
Lochailort (SR) 32B5
Locheilside (SR) 32B3
Lochgelly (SR) 320A3
Lochluichart (SR) 35C4
Lochwinnoch (SR) 29C3
Lockerbie (SR) 26A3
Lockwood (NT) 21E2/42D5
Lodge Road, West Bromwich Town Hall
   (Midland Metro) 13B2
(London) Blackfriars (FC) 40C5
(London) Cannon Street (NW) . . .5B3/40C4
(London) Charing Cross (NW) . . .5B3/40C5
(London) City Thameslink (FC) 40C5
(London) Euston (NW) 5A3/40C5
(London) Farringdon (LT) 40C5
(London) Fenchurch Street (NW) .5B3/40C4
(London) Kings Cross (NW) 5A3/40C5
(London) Kings Cross Thameslink (FC) .40C5
(London) Liverpool Street (NW) .5A3/40C4
(London) London Bridge (NW) . .5B3/40D4
(London) Marylebone (CH) 5A3/39C5
(London) Moorgate (LT) 40C4
(London) Paddington (NW) 5B3/39C5
(London) St Pancras (ML) 5A3/40C5
(London) Victoria (NW) 5A3/39D5
(London) Waterloo (NW) 5A3/40D5
(London) Waterloo (East) (SE) 40D5
London City Airport (DLR) 40C2
London Fields (LE) 40B4
London Road, Brighton (SN) 5F3
London Road, Guildford (SW) 5C1
Long Buckby (SL) 10B3
Long Eaton (CT) 16D4
Long Preston (NT) 24C1
Longbeck (NT) 28E3
Longbridge (CT) 9A4
Longcross (SW) 5B1
Longfield (SE) 5B5
Longniddry (SR) 30B1
Longport (CT) 15C3/20E1
Longton (CT) 15C3/20F1
Looe (GW) 1D4
Lostock (NT) 20B2/24F2/45C2
Lostock Gralam (NT) 15A2/20D2/45C5
Lostock Hall (NT) 20A3/24E3
Lostwithiel (GW) 1D3
Loughborough (CT) 16E4
Loughborough Central (Pres) 16E4
Loughborough Junction (FC) 40E5
Loughton (LT) 5A4
Lowdham (CT) 16C3
Lower Sydenham (SE) 40F3
Lowestoft (LE) 12A1/18G1
Loxdale (Midland Metro) 13A2
Ludlow (AW) 9A1
Luton (FC) 11E1
Luton Airport (FC) 11E1
Luxulyan (GW) 1D3
Lydney (GW) 8B1/9E2
Lye (CT) 9A3/15G3
Lymington Pier (SW) 4F4
Lymington Town (SW) 4F4
Lympstone Commando (GW) 2B3

Lympstone Village (GW) 2B3
Lytham (NT) 20A4/24E4

Macclesfield (VT) 15A3/20D1/45A5
Machynlleth (AW) 14B5
Maesteg (AW) 7B5/43E3
Maesteg Ewenny Road (AW) 7B5/43E3
Maghull (ME) 20B4/24F4/45F2
Maiden Newton (GW) 3F2/5B1
Maidenhead (GW) 4A1/12G2
Maidstone Barracks (SE) 6C5
Maidstone East (SE) 6C5
Maidstone West (SE) 6C5
Malden Manor (SW) 39G3
Malin Bridge (SYS) 42G2
Mallaig (SR) 32A5
Malton (TP) .22B5
Malvern Link (CT) 9C3
Manchester Airport (TP) . . .15A3/20C1/45B4
Manchester Oxford Road (NT) 45A3
Manchester Piccadilly (NW) 20B1/24F1/45A3
Manchester Victoria (NT) .20B1/24F1/45A3
Manea (LE) 11A3/17G3
Manningtree (LE) 12E4
Manor Park (LE) 40B2
Manor Road (ME) 20C5
Manorbier (AW) 7D2
Manors (NT) 28A1
Mansfield (CT) 16B4/41D4
Mansfield Woodhouse (CT) 16B4/41D4
Mansion House (LT) 40D5
March (LE) 11A3/17F3
Marden (SE) .6D5
Margate (SE) 6B1
Market Bosworth (Pres) 16F5
Market Harborough (ML) 16G2
Market Rasen (CT) 17A1/22G3
Markinch (SR) 30A2
Marks Tey (LE) 12E5
Marlow (GW) 10G2
Marple (NT) .21G1
Marsden (NT) 21F1
Marske (NT) .28E3
Marston Green (CT) 15G5
Martin Mill (SE) 6D1
Martins Heron (SW) 4A1
Marton (NT) .28E4
Maryhill (SR) 29C5/44E4
Maryland (LE) 40B2
Maryport (NT) 26D3
Matlock (CT) 16B5/41D1
Matlock Bath (CT) 16B5/41D1
Mauldeth Road (NT) 45A3
Maxwell Park (SR) 44E3
Maybole (SR) 29F3
Maze Hill (SE) 40D3
Meadowhall (NT; SYS) 21G3/42G2
Meadowhall South/Tinsley (SYS) 42G2
Medstead & Four Marks (Pres) 4C2
Meldreth (FC) 11D3
Melksham (GW) 3A4
Melton (LE) .12D3
Melton Mowbray (CT) 16E2
Mendip Vale (Pres) 3C3
Menheniot (GW) 1D4
Menston (NT) 21D2
Meols (ME) 20C5/24G5
Meols Cop (NT) 20A4/24E4/45F1
Meopham (SE) 5B5
Merryton (SR) 30D5/44B1

Merstham (SN) 5C3
Merthyr Tydfil (AW) 8A5/43C2
Merthyr Vale (AW) 8B5/43C2
Merton Park (CTL) 39F4
Metheringham (CT) 16B1/17B1
Metro Centre (NT) 28A2
Mexborough (NT) 21F4
Micheldever (SW) 4C3
Micklefield (NT) 21D4/42A1
Middlesbrough (TP) 28E4
Middlewood (NT) 15A4
Middlewood (SYS) 42G2
Midgham (GW) 4A3
Mile End (LT) 40C3
Milford (SW) 5D1
Milford Haven (AW) 7D1
Mill Hill (NT) 20A2/24E2
Mill Hill Broadway (FC) 5A2
Mill Hill East (LT) 5A3
Millbrook (Bedfordshire) (SL) 10C1
Millbrook (Hampshire) (SW) 4E4
Millfield (T&W) 28C5
Milliken Park (SR) 29C4
Millom (NT) 24A5
Mills Hill (NT) 20B1/24F1/45A2
Milngavie (SR) 29B5/44E5
Milnrow (NT) 20A1/45A1
Milton Keynes Central (SL) 10C2
Minehead (Pres) 8E5
Minffordd (AW) 19F2
Minster (SE) 6C2
Mirfield (NT) 21E2/42C4
Mistley (LE) 12E4
Mitcham (CTL) 39G5
Mitcham Junction (SN; CTL) 5B3/39G5
Mobberley (NT) 15A3/20C1/45B4
Monifieth (SR) 34E4
Monks Risborough (CH) 10E2
Monkseaton (T&W) 28B5
Montpelier (GW) 3A2
Montrose (SR) 34C2
Monument (LT) 40D4
Moor Bridge (NET) 41F4
Moorgate (LT) 40C4
Moorside (NT) 20B2/24F1/45B2
Moorthorpe (NT) 21F4/42D1
Morar (SR) 32B5
Morchard Road (GW) 2A4
Morden Road (CTL) 39F5
Morden South (FC) 39G4
Morecambe (NT) 24B3
Moreton (Dorset) (SW) 3F3
Moreton (Merseyside) (ME) 20C5/24G5
Moreton-in-Marsh (GW) 9D5
Morfa Mawddach (AW) 13A5
Morley (NT) 21D3/42B3
Morpeth (NT) 27A5
Mortimer (GW) 4A2
Mortlake (SW) 5B2/39E3
Moses Gate (NT) 20B2/24F2/45B2
Moss Side (NT) 24D4
Mossley (NT) 21F1
Mossley Hill (NT) 45F4
Mosspark (SR) 44F3
Moss Way (SYS) 41A3
Moston (NT) 20B1/24F1/45A2
Motherwell (SR) 30C5/44B2
Motspur Park (SW) 39G4
Mottingham (SE) 40E2
Mouldsworth (NT) 15B1/20D3/45D5

Moulscoomb (SN) 5F3
Mount Florida (SR) 44E3
Mount Vernon (SR) 44C3
Mountain Ash (AW) 8B5/43C2
Mudchute (DLR) 40D3
Muir of Ord (SR) 35D5
Muirend (SR) 29C5/44E2
Muncaster Mill (Pres) 26G3
Musselburgh (SR) 30B2
Mytholmroyd (NT) 21E1

Nafferton (NT) 22C3
Nailsea & Backwell (GW) 3A2/8D2
Nairn (SR) 36D4
Nantwich (AW) 15C2/20E2
Narberth (AW) 7D3
Narborough (CT) 16F4
Navigation Road (NT) 45B4
Neasden (LT) 39B4
Neath (AW) 7B4/43F2
Needham Market (LE) 12C4
Neilston (SR) 29C4/44G2
Nelson (NT) 24D1
Neston (AW) 20D4/45F5
Netherfield (CT) 16D3/41F5
Netherthorpe Road (SYS) 42G2
Nethertown (NT) 26F3
Netley (SW) 4E3
New Addington (CTL) 5C4
New Barnet (FC) 5A3/11G2
New Beckenham (SE) 40F3
New Brighton (ME) 20C4/24G4/45F4
New Clee (NT) 22F2
New Cross (SE) 40D3
New Cross Gate (SN) 40D3
New Cumnock (SR) 29F5
New Eltham (SE) 5B4/40E1
New Hey (NT) 21F1
New Holland (NT) 22E3
New Hythe (SE) 6C5
New Lane (NT) 20A4/24E3/45E1
New Malden (SW) 5B3/39F3
New Mills Central (NT) 15A4
New Mills Newtown (NT) 15A4
New Milton (SW) 4F5
New Pudsey (NT) 21D2/42A4
New Romney (Pres) 6E3
New Southgate (FC) 5A3
Newark Castle (CT) 16C2
Newark Northgate (GR) 16C2
Newbury (GW) 4A3
Newbury Park (LT) 40A1
Newbury Racecourse (GW) 4A3
Newby Bridge (Pres) 24A4
Newcastle (GR) 27B5/28A1
Newcastle Airport (T&W) 27B5
Newcraighall (SR) 30B2
Newhaven Harbour (SN) 5G4
Newhaven Town (SN) 5F4
Newington (SE) 6B4
Newmarket (LE) 11C4
Newport (Essex) (LE) 11E4
Newport (AW) 8B3/43A3
Newquay (GW) 1D1
Newstead (CT) 16C4/41E4
Newton (SR) 29C5/44C3
Newton Abbot (GW) 2C3
Newton Aycliffe (NT) 27E5
Newton for Hyde (NT) 21G1
Newton on Ayr (SR) 29F3

Newton St Cyres (GW) 2B3
Newton-le-Willows (NT) ..20C3/24G2/45D3
Newtondale Halt (Pres) 28G2
Newtonmore (SR) 33A2
Newtown (AW) 14C3
Ninian Park (AW) 43B4
Nitshill (SR) 29C4/44F3
Noel Street (NET) 41F4
Norbiton (SW) 5B2/39F3
Norbury (SN) 40F5
Norchard (Pres) 9E2
Norden (Pres) 3F4
Normans Bay (SN) 5F5
Normanton (NT) 21E3/42C2
North Acton (LT) 39C3
North Berwick (SR) 31B1
North Camp (GW) 4B1
North Dulwich (SN) 40E4
North Ealing (LT) 39C3
North Elmham (Pres) 18E4
North Llanrwst (AW) 19D3
North Queensferry (SR) 30B3
North Road (Darlington) (NT) 27E5
North Sheen (SW) 39E3
North Shields (T&W) 28B5
North Walsham (LE) 18D2
North Wembley (SL) 39B2
North Woolwich (SL) 5B4/40D1
Northallerton (TP) 21A3/28G5
Northampton (SL) 10B2
Northfield (CT) 9A4
Northfield (LT) 39D2
Northfleet (SE) 5B5
Northiam (Pres) 6F5
Northolt Park (CH) 39B2
Northumberland Park (LE) 40A4
Northwich (NT) 15A2/20D2/45C5
Northwood (Pres) 16B5/41D1
Norton Bridge (CT) 15D3/20G1
Norwich Thorpe (LE) 18F3
Norwood Junction (SN) 5B3/40G4
Notting Hill Gate (LT) 39C4
Nottingham (CT; NET) 16D3/41G5
Nuneaton (CT) 16G5
Nunhead (SE) 40D4
Nunnery Square (SYS) 41A2/42G2
Nunthorpe (NT) 28F4
Nutbourne (SN) 4E1
Nutfield (SE) 5D3

Oakamoor (Pres) 15C4
Oakengates (CT) 15E2
Oakham (CT) 16E2
Oakleigh Park (FC) 5A3/11G2
Oakworth (Pres) 21D1
Oban (SR) 32F4
Ockendon (CC) 5A5
Ockley (SN) 5D2
Okehampton (seasonal; Pres) 2C5
Old Hill (CT) 13A1/15G4
Old Roan (ME) 20B424F4/45F3
Old Street (LT) 40C4
Old Trafford (Metrolink) 45B3
Oldfield Park (GW) 8D1
Oldham Derker (NT) 21F1
Oldham Mumps (NT) 21F1
Oldham Werneth (NT) 20B1/21F1/45A2
Olton (CT) 9A5/15G5
Ore (SN) 6F5
Ormskirk (ME) 20B4/24F3/45E2

Orpington (SE) 5B4/40G1
Orrell (NT) 20B3/24F2/45D2
Orrell Park (ME) 45A3
Orton Mere (pres) 11A1/17F1
Osterley (LT) 39D2
Oswestry (Pres; proposed) 20G4
Otford (SE) 5C5
Oulton Broad North (LE) 12A1/18F1
Oulton Broad South (LE) 12A1/18G1
Outwood (NT) 21E3/42B2
Overpool (ME) 20D4/45F5
Overton (SW) 4B3
Oxenholme Lake District (VT) . . .24A3/27G1
Oxenhope (Pres) 21D1
Oxford (GW) 10E4
Oxshott (SW) 5C2
Oxted (SN) 5C4

Paddock Wood (SE) 5D5
Padgate (NT) 20C2/24G2/45C4
Paignton (GW) 2D3
Paisley Canal (SR) 29C4/44F4
Paisley Gilmour Street (SR) 29C4/44G4
Paisley St James (SR) 44G3
Pallion (T&W) 28C5
Palmers Green (FC) 5A1
Palmersville (T&W) 28B5
Pangbourne (GW) 4A2/10G3
Pannal (NT) 21C3
Pant (Pres) 8A5/43C1
Pantyffynnon (AW) 7A3/43G1
Par (GW) 1D3
Parbold (NT) 20B3/24F3/45E2
Park Lane Interchange (T&W) 28C5
Park Royal (LT) 39C3
Park Street (SL) 11G1
Parkend (Pres) 8A1/9E2
Parkstone (SW) 3F5
Parson Street (GW) 3A2
Parsons Green (LT) 39E4
Partick (SR) 44E4
Parton (NT) 26E4
Patchway (GW) 8C2/9G1
Patricroft (NT) 20B2/24F1/45B3
Patterton (SR) 29C4/44F2
Peartree (CT) 16D5/41G2
Peckham Rye (SN) 40D4
Pegswood (NT) 27A5
Pelaw (T&W) 28C5
Pemberton (NT) 20B3/24F3/45D2
Pembrey & Burry Port (AW) 7B2
Pembroke (AW) 7D2
Pembroke Dock (AW) 7D2
Penally (AW) 7D3
Penarth (AW) 8D4/43B5
Pencoed (AW) 43D4
Pengam (AW) 8B4/43B2
Penge East (SE) 40F4
Penge West (SN) 40F4
Penhelig (AW) 13B5
Penistone (NT) 21F3/42E3
Penkridge (CT) 15E3
Penmaenmawr (NT) 19D3
Penmere (AW) 1F1
Penrhiwceiber (AW) 8B5/43C2
Penrhyndeudraeth (Pres) 19F3
Penrith North Lakes (VT) 27E1
Penryn (AW) 1E1
Pensarn (AW) 19G2
Penshurst (SE) 5D4

Pentre-Bach (AW) 8B5/43C2
Pentrepiod Halt (Pres) 19F4
Pen-y-Bont (AW) 14D3
Penychain (AW) 19F1
Penyffordd (NT) 20E4
Pen-y-Mount (Pres) 19F2
Penzance (GW) 1F3
Percy Main (T&W) 28B5
Perranwell (GW) 1E1
Perry Barr (CT) 13B3
Pershore (GW) 9C4
Perth (SR) 33F5
Peterborough (GR) 11A2/17F2
Peterborough Town (Pres) . . .11A2/17F2
Petersfield (SW) 4D2
Petts Wood (SE) 40G1
Pevensey & Westham (SN) 5F5
Pevensey Bay (SN) 5F5
Pewsey (GW) 4B5
Phipps Bridge (CTL) 39F5
Phoenix Park (NET) 16C4/41F4
Pickering (Pres) 22A5
Pilning (GW) 8C2/9G1
Pinhoe (SW) 2C3
Pitlochry (SR) 33C4
Pitsea (CC) 6A5
Plaistow (LT) 40C2
Plas-y-nant (Pres) 19E2
Pleasington (NT) 20A2/24E2
Plockton (SR) 35E1
Pluckley (SE) 6D4
Plumley (NT) 15A2/20D2/45B5
Plumpton (SN) 5F3
Plumstead (SE) 40D1
Plymouth (GW) 1D5
Pokesdown (SW) 3F5
Polegate (SN) 5F5
Polesworth (CT) 16F5
Pollokshaws East (SR) 44E3
Pollokshaws West (SR) 44E3
Pollokshields East (SR) 44E3
Pollokshields West (SR) 44E3
Polmont (SR) 30B4
Polsloe Bridge (GW) 2B3
Ponders End (LE) 11G3
Ponlottyn (AW) 8A5/43C2
Pont Croesor (Pres) 19F2
Pontarddulais (AW) 7A3
Pontefract Baghill (NT) 21E4/42C1
Pontefract Monkhill (NT) 21E4/42C1
Pontefract Tanshelf (NT) 21E4/42C1
Pontlottyn (AW) 8A4/43C2
Pontsticill (Pres) 8A5/43C1
Pontyclun (AW) 43C4
Pontycymmer (Pres) 7B5
Pont-y-Pant (AW) 19E3
Pontypool & New Inn (AW) 8B3/43A2
Pontypridd (AW) 8B5/43C3
Poole (SW) 3F5
Poplar (DLR) 40C3
Poppleton (NT) 21C4
Port Erin (IoM) 23C1
Port Glasgow (SR) 29B3
Port Soderick (IoM) 23C2
Port St Mary (IoM) 23C1
Port Sunlight (ME) 45F4
Port Talbot Parkway (AW) 7B4/43F3
Portchester (SW) 4E3
Porth (AW) 8B5/43C3
Porthmadog (AW) 19F2

Portlethen (SR) 34A1/37G4
Portslade (SN) 5F3
Portsmouth & Southsea (SW) 4E2
Portsmouth Arms (GW) 7G3
Portsmouth Harbour (SW) 4E2
Possilpark & Parkhouse (SR) 44E4
Potters Bar (FC) 11G2
Poulton-le-Fylde (NT) 24D4
Poynton (NT) 15A3/20C1/45A4
Praed Street (LT) 39C5
Prees (GW) 15D1/20F3
Prescot (NT) 20C3/24G3/45E3
Prestatyn (AW) 19C5
Prestbury (NT) 15A3/20D1/45A5
Preston (VT) 20A3/24D3
Preston Park (SN) 5F3
Preston Road (LT) 39A3
Prestonpans (SR) 30B1
Prestwich (Metrolink) 20B1/20F1/45B2
Prestwick International Airport (SR) 29E3
Prestwick Town (SR) 29E3
Priestfield (Midland Metro) 13A1
Priesthill & Darnley (SR) 44F3
Prince Regent (DLR) 40C2
Princes Risborough (CH) 10F2
Prittlewell (LE) 6A4
Prudhoe (NT) 27C4
Pudding Mill Lane (DLR) 40B3
Pulborough (SN) 5E1
Purfleet (CC) 5B5
Purley (SN) 5C3
Purley Oaks (SN) 5C3
Putney (SW) 5B3/39E4
Putney Bridge (LT) 39E4
Pwllheli (AW) 19F1
Pyle (AW) 7C5

Quakers Yard (AW) 8B5/43C2
Queenborough (SE) 6B4
Queens Park (Glasgow) (SR) 44E3
Queens Park (London) (SL) 40B4
Queens Road (Peckham) (SN) 40D4
Queensbury (LT) 5A2
Queenstown Road (Battersea) (SW) 39D5
Quintrell Downs (GW) 1D1
Quorn & Woodhouse (Pres) 16E4

Radcliffe (CT) 16D3
Radcliffe (Metrolink) 20B1/20F1/45B2
Radford Road (NET) 41F4
Radlett (FC) 11G1
Radley (GW) 10F4
Radyr (AW) 8C4/43C4
Rainford (NT) 20B3/24F3/45E2
Rainham (Essex) 5A4
Rainham (Kent) 6B5
Rainhill (NT) 20C3/24G3//45E4
Ramsbottom (Pres) 20A1/24E1/45B1
Ramsey (IoM) 23B3
Ramsgate (SE) 6B1
Ramsgreave & Wilpshire (NT) 24D2
Rannoch (SR) 32D1/33C1
Rauceby (CT) 16C1/17C1
Ravenglass for Eskdale (NT) 26G3
Ravensbourne (SE) 40F3
Ravenscourt Park (LT) 39D4
Ravensthorpe (NT) 21E3/42C3
Rawcliffe (NT) 21E5
Rawtenstall (Pres) 20A1/24E1
Rayleigh (LE) 6A5

Rayners Lane (LT) 39B1
Raynes Park (SW) 5B3/39F4
Reading (GW) .4A2
Reading West (GW) 4A2
Rectory Road (LE) 40B4
Redbridge (SW) 4E4
Redcar British Steel (NT) 28E4
Redcar Central (NT) 28E3
Redcar East (NT) 28E3
Reddish North (NT) 45A3
Reddish South (NT) 45A3
Redditch (CT) .9A4
Redhill (SN) .5C3
Redland (GW) .3A2
Redmire (Pres) 21A1/27G4
Redruth (GW) 1E5
Reedham (Norfolk) (LE) 18F2
Reedham (Surrey) (SN) 5C3
Regent Centre (T&W) 27B5
Reigate (SN) 5C3
Renton (SR) .29B3
Retford (GR) 16A3
Rhiwbina (AW) 43B4
Rhoose (Cardiff International Airport)
    (AW) 8D5/43C5
Rhosneigr (AW) 19B2/19D1
Rhyd ddu (Pres) 19E2
Rhydyronen (Pres) 13B5
Rhyl (AW) 19C5
Rhymney (AW) 8A5/43C1
Ribblehead (NT) 24A1
Rice Lane (ME) 45A3
Richmond (SW) 5B2/39E3
Rickmansworth (LT) 5A2/10F1/11G1
Riddlesdown (SN) 5C3
Ridgmont (SL) 10C1
Riding Mill (NT) 27C4
Rishton (NT) 24D2
Robertsbridge (SE) 6F5
Roby (NT) 20C4/24G3/45E4
Rochdale (NT) 20B1/45A1
Roche (GW) .1D2
Rochester (SE) 6B5
Rochford (LE) 6A4
Rock Ferry (ME) 20C4/24G4/45F4
Roding Valley (LT) 5A4
Rogart (SR) .36A5
Rolleston (SR) 16C2
Rolvenden (Pres) 6E4
Roman Bridge (AW) 19E3
Romford (LE) 5A4
Romiley (NT) 21G1
Romney Sands (Pres) 6E3
Romsey (SW) 4D4
Ronaldsway Halt (IoM) 23C2
Roose (NT) .24B5
Ropley (Pres) 4C2
Rose Grove (NT) 24D1
Rose Hill Marple (NT) 21G1
Rosyth (SR) .30B3
Rotherham Central (NT) 21G4/42F1
Rotherhithe (LT) 40D4
Rothley (Pres) 16E4
Roughton Road (SR) 18D3
Rowlands Castle (SW) 4E2
Rowley Regis (CT) 13C2/G4
Rowsley (Pres) 16B5/41C1
Royal Oak (LT) 39C5
Roy Bridge (SR) 32B2
Royal Albert (DLR) 40C2

Royal Victoria (DLR) 40C2
Roydon (LE) 11F3
Royston (FC) 11D3
Ruabon (AW) 20F4
Ruddington (Pres) 16C4/41G4
Rufford (NT) 20A3/24E3/45E1
Rugby (VT) .10A4
Rugeley Town (CT) 15E4
Rugeley Trent Valley (CT) 15E4
Runcorn (VT) 15A1/20C3/45D4
Runcorn East (AW) 15A1/20C3/45D4
Ruskington (CT) 17C1
Ruswarp (NT) 28F2
Rutherglen (SR) 29C5/44D3
Ryde Espanade (IL) 4F3
Ryde Pier Head (IL) 4F3
Ryde St Johns Road (IL) 4F3
Ryder Brow (NT) 45A3
Rye (SN) 6E4
Rye House (LE) 11F3

St Albans (FC) 11F1
St Albans Abbey (SL) 11F1
St Andrews Road (GW) 8C2/9G1
St Anne's on the Sea (NT) 24D4
St Austell (GW) 1D2
St Bees (NT) 26F4
St Budeaux Ferry Road (GW) 1D5
St Budeaux Victoria Road (GW) 1D5
St Columb Road (GW) 1D2
St Denys (SW) 4D4
St Erth (GW) 1F4
St Germans (GW) 1D5
St Helens Central (NT) 20C3/24G3/45D3
St Helens Junction (NT) . .20C3/24G3/45D3
St Helier (FC) 39G4
St Ives (GW) 1E4
St James Park (GW) 2B3
St James' Park (LT) 40D5
St James Street (LE) 40A3
St Johns (SE) 40E3
St Johns Wood (LT) 39C5
St Keyne (GW) 1D4
St Leonards Warrior Square (SE) 6F5
St Margarets (Herts) (LE) 11F3
St Margarets (SW) 39E2
St Mary Cray (SE) 5B4/40G1
St Michaels (ME) 20C4/24G4/45F5
St Neots (FC) 11C2
St Pauls (Midland Metro) 13C3
St Peters (T&W) 28C5
Sale (Metrolink) 20C145B3
Salford Central (NT) 20B1/20F1/45B2
Salford Crescent (NT) 20B1/24F1/45B3
Salfords (SN) 5D3
Salhouse (LE) 18E2
Salisbury (SW) 4C5
Saltaire (NT) 21D2/42A5
Saltash (GW) 1D5
Saltburn (NT) 28E3
Saltcoats (SR) 29E3
Saltmarshe (NT) 22E5
Salwick (NT) 24D3
Sampford Courtenay (Pres) 2D5
Sandal & Agbrigg (NT) 21E3/42C2
Sandbach (NT) 15B2/20E2
Sanderstead (SN) 5C3
Sandhills (ME) 45F3
Sandhurst (GW) 4B1
Sandling (SE) 6D3

Sandown (IL) 4F3
Sandplace (GW) 1D4
Sandwell & Dudley (CT) 13B2
Sandwich (SE) 6C2
Sandy (FC) .11D2
Sankey for Penketh (NT) . .20C3//24G3/45D4
Sanquhar (SR) 30F5
Santon (IoM) 23C2
Sarn (AW) 7C5/43D4
Saundersfoot (AW) 7D3
Saunderton (CH) 10F2
Sawbridgeworth (LE) 11F3
Saxilby (CT) 16A1
Saxmundham (LE) 12C2
Scarborough (TP) 22A4/28G1
Scotscalder (SR) 38D3
Scotstounhill (SR) 29C4/44E4
Scunthorpe (TP) 22F4
Sea Mills (GW) 3A2/8C2/9G1
Seaburn (T&W) 28C5
Seaford (SN) 5G4
Selhurst (SN) 50B3/40G5
Seaforth & Litherland (ME) .20B4/24F4/45F3
Seaham (NT) 28C5
Seamer (TP) 22A3
Seascale (NT) 26F3
Seaton (Pres) 2B1
Seaton Carew (NT) 28E4
Seer Green (CH) 5A1/10F1
Selby (NT) .21D5
Selhurst (SN) 5B3/40G5
Sellafield (NT) 26F3
Selling (SE) .6C3
Selly Oak (CT) 9A4/15G4
Setons Halt (Pres) 18D5
Settle (NT) .24B1
Seven Kings (LE) 5A4
Seven Sisters (WN) 5A3/40A4
Sevenoaks (SE) 5C4
Severn Beach (GW) 8C2/9G1
Severn Tunnel Junction (AW) 8B2/9F1
Shackerstone (Pres) 16F5
Shadwell (LT) 40C4
Shalesmoor (SYS) 41A2/42G2
Shalford (GW) 5D1
Shanklin (IL) 4F3
Shaw & Compton (NT) 21F1
Shawford (SW) 4D3
Shawlands (SR) 44E3
Sheerness on Sea (SE) 6B4
Sheffield (ML) 16A5/21G3/41A2/42G2
Sheffield Park (Pres) 5E4
Sheffield Station (SYS) 42G2
Shelford (LE) 11D3
Shenfield (LE) 5A5/11G4
Shenstone (CT) 15F5
Shenton (Pres) 16F5
Shepherds Bush (LT) 39C4
Shepherds Bush (SL) 39C4
Shepherds Well (SE) 6C2
Shepley (NT) 21F2/42D4
Shepperton (SW) 5B2
Shepreth (FC) 11D3
Sherborne (SW) 3D3
Sherburn in Elmet (NT) 21D4
Sheringham (LE) 18C3
Shettleston (SR) 29C5/44D3
Shieldmuir (SR) 44A2
Shifnal (CT) 15F2
Shildon (NT) 27E5

Shiplake (GW) .10G2
Shipley (NT) 21D2/42A5
Shippea Hill (LE) 11B4
Shipton (GW) .10D5
Shirebrook (CT) 16B4/41C4
Shirehampton (GW) 3A2/8C2/9G1
Shiremoor (T&W) 28B5
Shireoaks (NT) 16A4/41A4
Shirley (CT) 9A5
Shoeburyness (CC) 6A4
Shoreditch (LT) 40C4
Shoreham (SE) .5C5
Shoreham by Sea (SN) 5F3
Shortlands (SE) 40F2
Shotton (AW) .20D4
Shotts (SR) 30C5
Shrewsbury (AW) 15E1
Sidcup (SE) 40E1
Sileby (CT) 16E3
Silecroft (NT) .24A5
Silkstone Common (NT) 21F3/42E3
Silver Street (LE) 5A3
Silverdale (NT) 24B3
Silvertown (SL) 40C2
Singer (SR) 44F5
Sittingbourne (SE) 6C4
Skegness (CT) .17B4
Skelmanthorpe (Pres) 21F3/42D3
Skewen (AW) 7B4/43F2
Skipton (CT) 21C1
Slade Green (SE) 5B4
Slaithwaite (NT) 21E2/42D5
Slateford (SR) .30B2
Sleaford (CT) 16C1/17C1
Sleights (NT) 28F2
Sloane Square (LT) 39D5
Slough (GW) 5B1/10G1
Smallbrook Junction (IL) 4F3
Small Heath (CT) 15G5
Smethwick Galton Bridge (CT) . .13B2/15G4
Smethwick Rolfe Street (CT) 13B2/15G4
Smitham (SN) .5C3
Smithy Bridge (NT) 20A1/421E1/5A1
Snaefell (IoM) .23B3
Snaith (NT) 21E5
Snaresbrook (LT) 5A4/40A2
Snodland (SE) .6C5
Snowdown Ranger (Pres) 19E2
Snowdown (SE) 6C2
Soho Benson Road (Midland Metro) . . .13C3
Sole Street (SE) 5B5
Solihull (CT) 9A5
Somerleyton (LE) 12A1/18F1
South Acton (SL) 39D3
South Bank (NT) 28E4
South Bermondsey (SN) 40D4
South Croydon (SN) 5C3
South Ealing (LT) 39D2
South Elmsall (NT) 21F4/42D1
South Gosforth (T&W) 27B5
South Greenford (GW) 39C2
South Gyle (SR) 30B3
South Hampstead (SL) 39B5
South Harrow (LT) 39B1
South Hylton (T&W) 28C5
South Kensington (LT) 39D5
South Kenton (SL) 39A2
South Shields (T&W) 28B5

South Merton (FC) 39G4
South Milford (NT) 21D4
South Quay (DLR) 40D3
South Ruislip (CH) 39B1
South Tottenham (SL) 40A4
South Wigston (CT) 16F4
South Woodford (LT) 5A4/40A2
Southall (GW) 5B2/39C1
Southampton Airport Parkway (SW) . . .4D3
Southampton Central (SW) 4E4
Southbourne (SN) 4E2
Southbury (LE) 11G3
Southease (SN) .5F4
Southend on Sea Central (CC) 6A4
Southend on Sea East (CC) 6A4
Southend on Sea Victoria (LE) 6A4
Southfields (LT) 39E4
Southminster (LE) 12G4
Southport (ME) 20A4/24E4/45F1
Southwick (SN) 5F3
Sowerby Bridge (NT) 21E1
Spalding (CT) .17E2
Spean Bridge (SR) 32B2
Spital (ME) 20C4/45F4
Spondon (CT) 16C5/41G2
Spooner Row (LE) 12A4/18F4
Spring Road (CT) 15G3
Springburn (SR) 44D4
Springfield (SR) 34F5
Squires Gate (NT) 24D4
Stadium of Light (T&W) 28C5
Stafford (VT) 15E3/20G1
Staines (SW) 5B2
Stallingborough (NT) 22F2
Stalybridge (NT) 21F1
Stamford (CT) 16F1/17F1
Stamford Brook (LT) 39D4
Stamford Hill (LE) 40A4
Stanford le Hope (CC) 5A5
Stanhope (Pres) 27D4
Stanlow & Thornton (NT) 45E5
Stanmore (LT) .AA2
Stansted Airport (LE) 11E4
Stansted Mountfitchet (LE) 11E4
Staplehurst (SE) 6D5
Stapleton Road (GW) 3A2/8C1
Starbeck (NT) .21C3
Starcross (GW) .2C3
Staveley (NT) .27G1
Staverton Bridge (Pres) 2D4
Stawberry Hill (SW) 5B2/39F2
Stechford (CT) .15G5
Steeton & Silsden (NT) 21C1
Stepney Green (LT) 40C3
Stepps (SR) 29C5/44C4
Stevenage (FC) 11E2
Stevenston (SR) 29E3
Stewartby (SL) 10C1
Stewarton (SR) 29D4
Stirling (SR) 30A5
Stockport (VT) 20C1/24G1/45A4
Stocksfield (NT) 27C4
Stocksmoor (NT) 21F2/42D4
Stockton (NT) .28E5
Stogumber (Pres) 8F5
Stoke Mandeville (CH) 10E2
Stoke Newington (LE) 40B4
Stoke on Trent (VT) 15C3/20F1
Stone (CT) 15D3/20F1
Stone Crossing (SE) 5B5

Stonebridge Park (SL) 39B3
Stonegate (SE) .5E5
Stonehaven (SR) 34A2
Stonehouse (GW) 9E3
Stoneleigh (SW) 5C3
Stourbridge Junction (CT) 9A3/15G3
Stourbridge Town (CT) 9A3/15G3
Stowmarket (LE) 12C4
Stranraer (SR) .25C2
Stratford (LE) .40B3
Stratford on Avon (CT) 9B5
Strathcarron (SR) 35E2
Streatham (SN) 40F5
Streatham Common (SN) 40F5
Streatham Hill (SN) 5B3/40E5
Streethouse (NT) 21E442C1
Stretford (Metrolink) 45B3
Strines (NT) 15A4/21G1
Stromeferry (SR) 35E1
Strood (SE) 6B5
Stroud (GW) 9E3
Stubbins (Pres) 20A1/24E1/45B1
Sturry (SE) 6C2
Styal (NT) 15A3/20C1/45A4
Sudbury & Harrow Road (CH) 39B2
Sudbury (LE) 12D5
Sudbury Hill, Harrow (CH) 39B2
Sudbury Hill (LT) 39B2
Sudbury Town (LT) 39B2
Sugar Loaf (AW) 14E4
Summerseat (Pres) 20A1/24E1/45B1
Summerston (SR) 44E4
Sunbury (SW) .5B2
Sunderland (NT/T&W) 28C5
Sundridge Park (SE) 40F2
Sunningdale (SW) 5B1
Sunnymeads (SW) 5B1
Surbiton (SW) 5B2/39G2
Surrey Quays (LT) 40D4
Sutton (Surrey) (SN) 5C3
Sutton Coldfield (CT) 15F5
Sutton Common (FC) 39G4
Sutton Parkway (CT) 16B4/41D4
Swale (SE) 6B4
Swanage (Pres) .3G5
Swanley (SE) 5B4
Swanscombe (SE) 5B5
Swansea (AW) 7B4/43G3
Swanwick (SW) 4E3
Sway (SW) 4E5
Swaythling (SW) 4D4
Swinderby (CT) 16B2
Swindon (GW) .9G5
Swineshead (CT) 17C2
Swinton (Greater Manchester)
   (NT) 20B1/24F1/45B2
Swinton (South Yorkshire) (NT) . .21F4/42F1
Swiss Cottage (LT) 39B5
Sydenham (SN) 40F4
Sydenham Hill (SE) 40F4
Sylfaen (Pres) .14B2
Syon Lane (SW) 5B2/39D2
Syston (CT) 16E3

Tackley (GW) .10D4
Tadworth (SN) .5C3
Taff's Well (AW) 8C4/43C4
Tain (SR) 36B4
Tal-y-Cafn (AW) 19D4
Talsarnau (AW) 19F2

Talybont (AW) 19B2
Tame Bridge Parkway (CT) 13B3/15F4
Tamworth (CT) 15F5
Tan-y-Bwlch (Pres) 19F3
Tan-y-Grisau (Pres) 19F3
Taplow (GW) 5B1/10G2
Tattenham Corner (SN) 5C3
Taunton (GW) 8F4
Taynuilt (SR) 32E3
Teddington (SW) 5B2/39F2
Tees-side Airport (NT) 28F5
Teignmouth (GW) 2C3
Telford Central (CT) 15E2
Temple (LT) 40D5
Templecombe (SW) 3D3/8G1
Tenby (AW) 7D3
Tenterden Town (Pres) 6D4
Teynham (SE) 6C4
Thames Ditton (SW) 5B239G2
Thatcham (GW) 4A3
Thatto Heath (NT) 20C3/24G3/45E3
The Crescent (Midland Metro) 13A1
The Forest (NET) 41F4
The Green (Pres) 26F2
The Hawthorns (CT) 13B3
The Lakes (CT) 9A5
The Midden (Pres) 18C5
Theale (GW) 4A2
Theobalds Grove (LE) 11G3
Therapia Lane (CTL) 40G5
Thetford (LE) 12A4/18G5
Theydon Bois (LT) 11G3
Thirsk (TP) 21A4
Thornaby (TP) 28E4
Thorne North (NT) 21E5
Thorne South (NT) 21F5
Thornford (GW) 3E2
Thornliebank (SR) 29C5/44E2
Thornton Abbey (NT) 22E3
Thornton Heath (SN) 5BB3/40G5
Thorntonhall (SR) 29D5/44E2
Thorpe Bay (CC) 6A4
Thorpe Culvert (CT) 17B4
Thorpe-le-Soken (LE) 12E3
Three Bridges (SN) 5D3
Three Oaks (SN) 6F5
Thurgarton (CT) 16C3
Thurnscoe (NT) 21F4/42E1
Thurso (SR) 38C3
Thurston (LE) 12C5
Tilbury Town (CC) 5B5
Tile Hill (CT) 10A5
Tilehurst (GW) 4A2/10G3
Timperley (Metrolink) 20C1/20G1/45B3
Tipton (CT) 13B2/15F4
Tir-phil (AW) 8B4/43B2
Tisbury (SW) 3D4
Tiverton Parkway (GW) 2A2/8G5
Toddington (Pres) 9D4
Todmorden (NT) 20A1/21E1
Tolworth (SW) 5C2
Ton Pentre (AW) 43D2
Tonbridge (SE) 5D5
Tondu (AW) 7C5/43D4
Tonfanau (AW) 13B5
Tonypandy (AW) 8B5/43D3
Tooting (FC) 39F5
Topsham (GW) 2B3
Torpantau (Pres) 8A5/43C1
Torquay (GW) 2D3

Torre (GW) 2D3
Totnes (GW) 2D4
Totnes (Littlehempston) (Pres) 2D4
Tottenham Hale (LE) 40A4
Totteridge (LT) 5A3/11G2
Totton (SW) 4E4
Tower Gateway (DLR) 40C4
Town Green (ME) 20B4/24F4/45F2
Trafford Park (NT) 20C1/24G1/45B3
Trefforest (AW) 8B5/43C3
Trefforest Estate (AW) 43C3
Trehaford (AW) 8B5/43C3
Treherbert (AW) 8B5/43D2
Treorchy (AW) 43D2
Trimley (LE) 12E3
Tring (SL) 10E1
Troed-y-Rhiw (AW) 43C2
Troon (SR) 29E3
Trowbridge (GW) 3B4
Truro (GW) 1E1
Tulloch (SR) 32B1
Tulse Hill (SN) 5B3/40E5
Tunbridge Wells (SE) 5D5
Turkey Street (LE) 11G3
Turnham Green (LT) 39D3
Tutbury & Hatton (CT) 15D5
Twickenham (SW) 5B3/39E2
Twyford (GW) 4A1/12G2
Ty Croes (AW) 19D1
Ty Glas (AW) 43B4
Tygwyn (AW) 19F2
Tyndrum Lower (SR) 32E1
Tynemouth (T&W) 28B5
Tyseley (CT) 15G5
Tywyn (AW) 13B5
Tywyn Pendre (Pres) 13B5
Tywyn Wharf (Pres) 13B5

Uckfield (SN) 5E4
Uddingston (SR) 29C5/44C3
Ulceby (NT) 22E3
Ulleskelf (NT) 21D4
Ulverston (TP) 24A4
Umberleigh (GW) 7F3
University (CT) 13C3
University (T&W) 28C5
University of Sheffield (SYS) 42G2
Uphall (SR) 30C3
Upholland (NT) 20B3/24F3/45D2
Upminster (CC) 5A5
Upper Halliford (SW) 5B2
Upper Holloway (SL) 39B5
Upper Tyndrum (SR) 32E1
Upper Warlingham (SN) 5C3
Upton (AW) 20C4/24G4/45F4
Upton Park (LT) 40B2
Upwey (SW) 3G3
Urmston (NT) 20C1/24G1/45B3
Uttoxeter (CT) 15D5
Uxbridge (LT) 5A2

Valley (AW) 19B2
Valley Centertainment (SYS) 42G2
Vauxhall (SW) 40D5
Virginia Water (SW) 5B1

Waddon (SN) 5C3
Waddon Marsh (CTL) 40G5
Wadhurst (SE) 5E5
Wainfleet (CT) 17C4

Wainhill (Pres) 10F2
Wakefield Kirkgate (NT) 21E3/42C2
Wakefield Westgate (GR) 21E3/4C2
Walkden (NT) 20B2/24F1/45B2
Wallasey Grove Road (ME) .20C4/24G4/45F4
Wallasey Village (ME) 20C4/24G4/45G4
Wallingford (Pres) 10F3
Wallington (SN) 5C3
Wallsend (T&W) 28B5
Wallyford (SR) 30B1
Walmer (SE) 6C1
Walsall (CT) 15F4
Walsden (NT) 21E1
Walsingham (Pres) 18D5
Waltham Cross (LE) 11G3
Walthamstow Central (LE) 40A3
Walthamstow Queens Road (SL) 40A3
Walton on Naze (LE) 12E3
Walton (Merseyside) (ME) 45F3
Walton on Thames (SW) 5C2
Wanborough (SW) 5C1
Wandsworth Common (SN) 39E5
Wandsworth Road (SN) 40E5
Wandsworth Town (SW) 39E5
Wansford (Pres) 11A1/17F1
Wanstead Park (SL) 40B2
Wapping (LT) 40C4
Warblington (SN) 4E2
Warcop (Pres) 27E2
Ware (LE) 11F3
Wareham (SW) 3F4
Wargrave (GW) 4A1/12G2
Warham Halt (Pres) 18D5
Warminster (GW) 3C4
Warnham (SN) 5D2
Warrington (VT/NW) ...20C2/24G2/45D4
Warrington Bank Quay (VT) 45D4
Warrington Central (TP) 45D4
Warwick (CH) 10B5
Warwick Parkway (CH) 10B5
Washford (Pres) 8E5
Watchet (Pres) 8E5
Water Orton (CT) 15F5
Waterbeach (FC) 11C4
Wateringbury (SE) 6C5
Waterloo (Merseyside) (ME) 20B4/24F4/45F3
Waterston 7D1
Waterthorpe (SYS) 41A3
Watford High Street (SL) 5A1
Watford Junction (SL) 5A1
Watford North (SL) 11G1
Watlington (FC) 17E4
Watton at Stone (FC) 11F2
Waun-gron Park (AW) 43B4
Wedgwood (CT) 15D3/20F1
Wednesbury Great Western Street
  (Midland Metro) 13B2
Wednesbury Parkway (Midland Metro) .13B2
Weeley (LE) 12E3
Weeton (NT) 21C3
Welham Green (FC) 11F2
Welling (SE) 5B4
Wellingborough (ML) 10B2
Wellington (Shropshire) (CT) 15E1
Wells (Pres) 18C5
Welshpool (AW) 14B2
Welshpool Raven Square (Pres) 14B2
Welwyn Garden City (FC) 11F2
Welwyn North (FC) 11F2
Wem (AW) 15D1/20G3

Wembley Central (SL) 5A2/39B2
Wembley Park (LT) 39B3
Wembley Stadium (CH) 39B3
Wemyss Bay (SR) 29C2
Wendover (CH) 10E2
Wennington (NT) 24B2
West Acton (LT) 39C3
West Allerton (NT) 45E4
West Brompton (LT) 39D5
West Bromwich Central
    (Midland Metro) 13B2
West Byfleet (SW) 5C1
West Calder (SR) 30C4
West Croydon (SN) 5C3
West Drayton (GW) 10G1
West Dulwich (SE) 40E4
West Ealing (GW) 39C2
West Ferry (DLR) 40C3
West Ham (SL) 40C5
West Hampstead (SL) 39B5
West Hampstead Thameslink (FC) 39B5
West Harrow (LT) 39A1
West Horndon (CC) 5A5
West India Quay (DLR) 40C3
West Jesmond (T&W) 27B5/28A1
West Kensington (LT) 39D4
West Kilbride (SR) 29D2
West Kirby (ME) 20C5/24G5
West Malling (SE) 5C5
West Monkseaton (T&W) 28B5
West Norwood (SN) 40F5
West Ruislip (CH) 10G1
West Runton (LE) 18C3
West St Leonards (SE) 6F5
West Silvertown (DLR) 40C2
West Sutton (FC) 5C3
West Wickham (SE) 5B4/40G3
West Worthing (SN) 5F2
Westbourne Park (LT) 39C5
Westbury (GW) 3B4
Westcliff (CC) 6A4
Westcombe Park (SE) 40D2
Westenhanger (SE) 6D3
Wester Hailes (SR) 30C3
Westerfield (LE) 12D3
Westfield (SYS) 41A3
Westerton (SW) 44E5
Westgate-on-Sea (SE) 6B2
Westhoughton (NT) 20B2/24F2/45C2
Westminster (LT) 40D5
Weston Milton (GW) 3B1/8D3
Weston super Mare (GW) 3B1/8D3
Wetheral (NT) 27C1
Weybourne (Pres) 18C4
Weybridge (SW) 5C2
Weymouth (SW) 3G3
Whaley Bridge (NT) 15A4
Whalley (NT) 24D2
Whatstandwell (CT) 16C5/41E2
Whifflet (SR) 30C5/44B3
Whimple (SW) 2B2
Whinhill (SR) 29B3
Whiston (NT) 20C3/24G3/45E4
Whitby (NT) 28F2
Whitchurch (Cardiff) (AW) 43B4
Whitchurch (Hants) (SW) 4B3

Whitchurch (Salop) (AW) 20F3
White City (LT) 39C4
White Hart Lane (LE) 40A4
White Lane (SYS) 41A2
White Notley (LE) 11F5
Whitechapel (LT) 40C4
Whitecraigs (SR) 29C5/44E2
Whitefield (Metrolink) 20B1/20F1/45B2
Whitehaven (NT) 26E4
Whitland (AW) 7A1/13G3
Whitley Bay (T&W) 28B5
Whitley Bridge (NT) 21A5
Whitlock's End (CT) 9A5
Whitstable (SE) 6B3
Whittlesea (LE) 17G2
Whittlesford (LE) 11D3
Whitton (SW) 5B2/39E1
Whitwell (CT) 16A4/41B4
Whyteleafe (SN) 5C3
Whyteleafe South (SN) 5C3
Wick (SR) 38D2
Wickford (LE) 6A5
Wickham Market (LE) 12C2
Widdrington (NT) 27A5/31G5
Widnes (NT) 15A1/20C3/24G3/45D4
Widney Manor (CT) 9A5
Wigan (VT/NT) 20B3/24F2/45D2
Wigan North Western (VT) 45D2
Wigan Wallgate (NT) 45D2
Wigton (NT) 26C2
Wildmill (NT) 7C5/43D4
Wilkinson Street (NET) 41F4
Willesden Green (LT) 39D4
Willesden Junction (SL) 5A3/39C4
Williamwood (SR) 44E2
Willington (CT) 16D5
Williton (Pres) 8E5
Wilmcote (CT) 9B5
Wilmslow (NT) 15A3/20C1/45A5
Wilnecote (CT) 15F5
Wimbledon (SW) 5B3/39F4
Wimbledon Chase (FC) 39F4
Wimbledon Park (LT) 39E4
Winchcombe (Pres) 9D4
Winchelsea (SN) 6E4
Winchester (SW) 4D3
Winchfield (SW) 4B1
Winchmore Hill (FC) 5A1
Windermere (TP) 26G1
Windermere Lakeside (Pres) 24A4
Windsor & Eton Central (GW) 5B1
Windsor & Eton Riverside (SW) 5B1
Winnersh (SW) 4B1
Winnersh Triangle (SW) 4A1
Winsford (CT) 15B2/20D2
Winson Green, Outer Circle
    (Midland Metro) 13C3
Wirksworth (Pres) 16C5/41E1
Witham (LE) 11F5
Wisbech (Pres; proposed) 17F3
Wishaw (SR) 30C5/44A2
Witley (SW) 5D1
Wittersham Road (Pres) 6E4
Witton (CT) 13B4
Wivelsfield (SN) 5E3
Wivenhoe (LE) 12E4

Woburn Sands (SL) 10C1
Woking (SW) 5C1
Wokingham (SW) 4A1
Woldingham (SN) 5C3
Wolsingham (Pres) 27D5
Wolverhampton (VT) 15F3
Wolverton (SL) 10C2
Wombwell (NT) 21F3/42E2
Wood End (CT) 9A5
Wood Street (LE) 40A3
Woodbridge (LE) 12D3
Woodburn Road (SYS) 41A2/42G2
Woodgrange Park (SL) 40B2
Woodhall (SR) 29B3
Woodham Ferrers (LE) 11G5
Woodhouse (NT) 16A4/21G4/41A3/42G1
Woodlands Road (Metrolink) 45A2
Woodlesford (NT) 21D3/42B2
Woodley (NT) 21G1
Woodmansterne (SN) 5C3
Woodside (CTL) 40G4
Woodsmoor (NT) 21G1
Wool (SW) 3F4
Woolston (SW) 4E4
Woolwich Arsenal (SE) 40D1
Woolwich Dockyard (SE) 5B4/40D2
Wootton (Pres) 4F3
Wootton Wawen (CT) 9B5
Worcester Foregate Street (CT) 9B3
Worcester Park (SW) 5B3/39G4
Worcester Shrub Hill (CT) 9B3
Workington (NT) 26E3
Worksop (NT) 16A3/41B5
Worle (GW) 3A1/8D3
Worplesdon (SW) 5C1
Worstead (LE) 18E2
Worthing (SN) 5F2
Wrabness (LE) 12E3
Wraysbury (SW) 5B1
Wrenbury (AW) 15C2/20E3
Wressle (NT) 21D5
Wrexham Central (AW) 20E4
Wrexham General (AW) 20E4
Wye (SE) .6D3
Wylam (NT) 27B5
Wylde Green (CT) 15F5
Wymondham (LE) 18F4
Wythall (CT) 9A5

Yalding (SE) 5C5
Yardley Wood (CT) 9A5
Yarm (TP) 28F5
Yate (GW) 9G2
Yatton (GW) 3A1/8D3
Yeoford (GW) 2B2
Yeovil Junction (SW) 3E2/8G2
Yeovil Pen Mill (GW) 3D2/8G2
Yetminster (GW) 3E2
Ynyswen (AW) 8B5/43D2
Yoker (SR) 29C4/44F4
York (GR) 21C5
Yorton (GW) 15E1/20G3
Ystrad Mynach (AW) 8B4/43B3
Ystrad Rhondda (AW) 43D2

INDEX OF FREIGHT AND OTHER NON-PASSENGER TERMINALS

Note: A number of these locations are no longer regularly served although the route remains intact but disused. These locations, such as Portishead, are shown for the sake of completeness.

Aberdeen Waterloo 37G4
Aberthaw .8D5/43C5
Alexandra Dock 43A4
Allerton Bywater 42B1
Angerstein Wharf 40D2
Ardingly 5E3
Auchmuchty 34G5
Baddesley 15F5
Baglan Bay 45F3
Barton Hill 3G1
Bates Staithes 28A5
Bentinck 41E3
Berkeley 8B1/9F2
Birmingham Lawley Street 13C4
Blyth 28A5
Bolsover 16B4/41C3
Boulby 28E2
Bournemouth West 3F5
Brackmills 10B2
Bredbury 45A3
Brentford Goods 39D2
Bridge Street .10B2
Bridgend Engine Works 7C5/43D4
Broomhill 29F4
Brownhills 15F4
Brunt Hill 26C1
Burghead 36C2
Burn Naze 24D4
Butterworth 27A5
Cardiff Docks .8C4
Caerwent 8B2/9F1
Caldon Low 15C5
Calverton 16C3/41E4
Cardiff Docks .43B5
Carlisle London Road 26D1
Cattewater 1D5
Chalmerston 29G4
Clipstone Colliery 16B3
Coalville 16E4
Colnbrook 5B1/10G1
Corby 16G1
Cottam 16A2
Cowley 10E4
Cronberry 29F5
Cwm 54C4
Cwm Bargoed 8A5/43C2
Cwmgwrach 43E2
Cwmmawr 7A3
Cymgwrach 7A5/43E2
Deanside Transit 44F4
Denby 16C5/41F2
Devonport Docks 1A1
Dewsbury Stone Terminal 42C3
Drax 21E5
Drinnick Mill 1D2
Dudley 13B1
Dungeness Power Station 6E3
East Leake 16D4
Edwalton 16C3/41G5

Edwinstowe 41C5
Elgin East 36C2
Ellington/Lynemouth 28A5
Fawley 4E3
Felixstowe Docks 12E3
Fen Drayton .11B2
Fidlers Ferry 15A1/20C3/24G3/45D4
Fifoots .8C3/43A4
Flixborough 22F5
Fowey 1D3
Furzebrook 3F4
Gedling 16C3/41F5
Giffen 29D3
Grangemouth .30B4
Gwaun Cae Gurwen 7A4/43F1
Hamworthy Goods 3F5
Hartlepool Docks 28D4
Harworth 21G5
Heathfield 2C4
Highgate Wood Sidings 39A4
Hindlow 15A5
Horrocksford .24D1
Hull Botanic Gardens 22A1
Hull Dairycoates 22A2
Hull King George Dock 22E3
Hunslet East .42A2
Immingham Docks 22E2
Ipswich Griffin Wharf 12D3
Ipswich Lower Yard 12D3
Ironbridge Power Station 15F2
Killingholme .22E3
Killoch 29F4
Kincardine 30A4
Kineton 10B5
Latchford 15A2/20C2/24G2/45C4
Long Marston 9C5
Longbridge 9A4
Longtown 26B1
Ludgershall 4B5
Machen 8A4/43B3
Manisty Wharf 45E5
Marchwood 4E4
Marsh Barton .2B3
Maxwelltown .26B4
Meldon Quarry 2B5
Merehead 3C3
Methil 30A2/34G5
Middlesbrough Wharf 28E4
Middleton Towers 17E5
Millerhill 30C2
Monk Bretton 21F3/42E2
Moorfields 9C1
Moorswater 1D4
Moreton-on-Lugg 9C1
North Blyth 28A5
Old Dalby 14D3
Onllwyn 7A5/43E1
Oxcroft 16A4/41B3
Parkandillack .1D2

Partington 20C2/24G1/45B3
Peak Forest 15A5
Pig's Bay 6E4
Plymouth Friary 1D5
Pontycymer 7B5/43D3
Port Clarence .28E4
Portishead 8C2/9G1
Powderhall 30F2
Radstock 3B3/8E1
Ramsden Dock 24B5
Robeston 7D1
Round Oak 15G3
Roxby 22E4
Royal Portbury Dock 3A2/8C2
Rufford Quarry 16B4/41D5
Runcorn ICI Works 15A1
Rylstone 21C1
Scunthorpe Steelworks 22F4
Seal Sands 28E4
Seaton on Tees 28E4
Sellafield BNF 26F3
Sharpness 8B1/9F2
Shut End 15G3
Silverwood 42F1
Sinfin 16D5
Sizewell 12C2
Skinningrove .28E3
South Leith 30F1
Southampton East Docks 4E4
Stanton 41G3
Stewarts Lane 39F4
Stocksbridge 21F3/42F3
Stranraer Town 25C2
Stratton 9F5
Sudbrook 8B2/9F1
Swansea Docks 43G3
Tanhouse Lane 15A1/20C3/45D4
Thameshaven .6A5
Thamesport 6B4
Thoresby Colliery 16D3
Thrybergh 42F1
Tilbury Riverside 5B2
Tinsley 21G4/42G2
Tollerton 16D3
Toton 41G3
Tower .8A5/43D2
Trawsfynydd .19F3
Trecwn 13F1
Tytherington 8B1/9F3
Wardley 28C5
Waterside 29F4
Waterston 7D1
Welbeck Colliery 16B3/41C5
Welsh Westerleigh 8C1/9G2
Westfield 30A2
Whatley Quarry 3B3/8E1
Whitemoor 11A3/17F3
Winnington 15A2/20D3/45C5